Judaism
Key Facts

CHABAD HOUSE

© Rabbi N.D. Dubov, 2002
All Rights Reserved

First published in 2002 by
CHABAD HOUSE,
42 S. George's Road,
London, SW19 4ED

ISBN 0 9541655 1 9

Typeset by
Hames Publishing, London

Printed & bound in the UK by
Cox & Wyman, Reading

Contents

1 Proof of the Existence of G-d — 1

2 What is Life's Purpose? — 31

3 The Chosen People; Chosen for What? — 52

4 Why is Life so Difficult? — 58

5 What is the Secret of Jewish Survival? — 67

6 Can One Be a Good Jew Without Being Religious? — 80

7 Are Science and Religion a Contradiction? — 96

8 What is Wrong With Intermarriage? — 120

9 What is the Role of the Woman in Judaism? — 141

10 Belief After the Holocaust — 151

11 How Does One Cope With Bereavement? — 168

12 What is the Jewish Belief About "The End of Days"? — 173

13 Doing or Understanding – Which Comes First? — 183

Epilogue The Ten *Mitzvah* Campaigns — 193

Glossary — 199

This book is dedicated in memory of our dear parents
Miriam (Mae) and Marcus (Mick) Katz
of blessed memory
and
David and Ada Zetland
of blessed memory

Jacquie and Stuart Katz

Introduction

With gratitude to the A–mighty, I am delighted to present *Judaism Key FAQs* – questions and answers exploring the very core of Judaism.

The essays presented herein are based on the works of the Lubavitcher Rebbe, Rabbi Menachem Mendel Schneerson, drawing from his public talks (*Sichot*) and his private correspondence (*Igrot*). Relevant material and anecdotes gleaned from years of *Shlichus* experience have been added.

It is my fervent hope that this book will persuade and encourage the reader to lead a life dedicated to Torah and *mitzvot*, and hasten the coming of *Mashiach*, speedily, Amen.

My heartfelt thanks go to Stuart and Jacquie Katz who have so generously dedicated this book in memory of their parents. May Hashem bless them with all that is good both materially and spiritually.

A warm word of gratitude to all those who have edited the text, especially to my esteemed colleagues Rabbi Philip Ginsbury MA, Rabbi Z.H. Telsner, and Rabbi C. Rapoport MA. Thanks also to Mrs. Y. Saunders for her research.

Special thanks to my wife and children for all their support and encouragement in our joint *Shlichus*.

Rabbi Nissan Dovid Dubov
Director – Chabad Lubavitch of South London
Chabad House, Wimbledon
19 Kislev 5763

1

Proof of the Existence of G–d

"Prove to me that G–d exists" is a challenge as old as religion itself. Religion is defined as a belief in the existence of a superhuman controlling power, and when we give Judaism as our religion our belief in G–d is axiomatic. Yet so many Jews still question this very foundation.

It is still more difficult to articulate a convincing response. Furthermore, any answer is usually followed by a torrent of protest questioning such a belief, like the questions, "if there is a G–d, where was He during the Holocaust?", and, "why do bad things happen to good people?" In this chapter, we shall focus on the core issue.

Before doing so, we shall state briefly the Jewish belief in G–d. Many Jews recite daily the Thirteen Principles of Faith, based on the commentary of Maimonides to *Mishnah Sanhedrin* 10:1. The first four principles are:

1. I believe with complete faith that the Creator, blessed be His name, is the Creator and Guide of all the created beings, and that He alone has made, does make, and will make all things.
2. I believe with complete faith that the Creator,

blessed be His name, is One and Alone; that there is no oneness in any way like Him; and that He alone is our G–d – was, is, and will be.

3. I believe with complete faith that the Creator, blessed be His name, is incorporeal; that He is free from all anthropomorphic properties; and that He has no likeness at all.

4. I believe with complete faith that the Creator, blessed be His name, is the first and the last.

Prove the existence of G–d? In truth we must analyse the question before we attempt an answer. What is considered a proof? How does one prove that anything exists? Take, for example, a blind man. Does colour exist for the blind man? He cannot see colour yet it still exists. That fact is established by others who can see. The blind man believes and trusts that his fellow men can see that colour does exist although it is beyond his personal experience.

For a further example, take electricity. When we turn on a light can we see electricity? The answer is no, we see only its effect. Take gravity. When an object falls we cannot see, hear, feel, taste or smell gravity – we see only its effect. All agree that gravity is an undisputed fact of nature – since we see its effect. Scientists today are still baffled as to exactly what is the "stuff" of gravity.

In short, the proof of existence of any matter does not necessarily mean that we have to sense it in any way. It exists because we see its effect or, as in the case of the

Proof of the Existence of G–d

blind man, we believe others who can see it. G–d, we believe, does not have a body or form of body. He is everywhere and creates time and space. By definition, we cannot transcribe any physical description to G–d. By definition, man cannot actually see G–d. In order, therefore, to prove the existence of G–d we must rely either on seeing His effect ourselves, or on others who have seen His effect (like the blind man).

To summarise, proving the existence of G–d may be done in two ways. First, by examining whether anyone has actually witnessed something Divine or, secondly, by extrapolating proof of existence from His effect. To express it slightly differently, by tradition or by metaphysical proof. We shall also examine proof of existence by studying Jewish history and the fulfilment of prophecy.

Before we examine all these avenues it must be mentioned that the great Jewish philosophers disagreed as to which is the strongest proof. Rabbi Yehuda Halevi in his book *Kuzari* (2:26) argues that, "the highest faith is that derived through tradition alone, in which case metaphysical proof should only be used as a last resort to preclude disbelief." Maimonides (*Moreh Nevuchim* 3:51) disagrees. He argues that, "our faith begins with the traditions that have been transmitted to us by our ancestors and in our sacred literature. This is alluded to in the verse, 'Hear O Israel, G–d is our L–rd, G–d is one.' However, the highest level of faith comes from philosophical proof, and those who have the ability are required to prove the foundations of our faith."

In this essay we shall examine all avenues. Our approach is that, through a combination of traditional, philosophical and historical proofs, any thinking Jew will be led to a firm faith in the existence of G–d.

The traditional proof

In a court of law the strongest proof that something happened or existed is a witness statement. Seeing is believing. You cannot compare something seen to something heard.

Any historical fact is proven by those who witnessed and recorded the event. It follows that the more witnesses to that event, the more *bona fide* the fact.

One of the most celebrated holidays in the Jewish calendar is Passover. On *Seder* night Jews all over the world gather in family groups to recall the Exodus from Egypt. The evening is full of ritual and the *Haggadah* is our guide. One thing common to all is the eating of *matzah* – the bread of affliction. The Zohar (an early Kabbalistic work) calls *matzah* the bread of faith. It reminds us that the Jews ate *matzah* upon leaving Egypt. Although customs may differ, the basic story of the Exodus remains the same. Jews from Bombay, Birmingham or Belarus all tell the same story.

Ask any Jew how many plagues there were in Egypt and his answer would be 10. If anyone suggested there were 11, he would immediately be contradicted, not just by the historical detail, as presented in the Torah, but primarily because of the yearly re-enactment of the Ten Plagues at the *Seder*. We have a custom of spilling some of the wine at the mention of each plague. We would have remembered if there were 11 plagues. No, there were 10.

In fact, had there been "Chinese whispers", a distortion of the story over generations, we would have ended up with different versions of the story. All agree, however, that the Jews left Egypt and, forty-nine days later, stood before Mount Sinai and heard the Ten Commandments from G–d.

This is known, not just because a book (the Torah) tells us so, but simply by tradition – by the fact that generation after generation of Jews have transmitted this story, and that it is based on the actual experience of an entire nation. It therefore remains an undisputed historical fact. The Jews who left Egypt witnessed the Ten Plagues, the Exodus, and revelation at Sinai, and transmitted these events down the generations.

Throughout Jewish history there were never less than approximately a million Jews who transmitted this tradition, and the basic story remained the same even when the Jews were dispersed and scattered to the four corners of the earth. At Sinai, 600,000 men between the ages of 20 and 60, plus women and children (and men under the age of 20 and over the age of 60) – a total of approximately three million people – heard the Ten Commandments from G-d Himself. This event, recorded in the Torah, is, at the same time, a witnessed event of history and therefore an undisputed historical fact. To discredit it is highly unscientific.

It must be stressed that the revelation at Sinai was unlike any other revelation claimed by any other religion. In Christianity, revelation is assigned to one man or to a small group of disciples, and the same is true in Islam (to Mohammed) and Buddhism (to an ancient Hindu sage, the Buddha – enlightened one – whose followers adopted his teachings and doctrines and called themselves Buddhists after him). Not so in Judaism – the revelation was to an entire nation.

In fact, a great rabbi, Rabbi Shlomo Ben Aderet (*Rashba*), explains that the stand at Sinai was necessary because if revelation had been only to one man – Moshe – it would have been disputed. He explains: imagine Moshe coming to Egypt and telling the Jews that the time for their redemption had arrived. At first they doubt him, but once he begins to bring about the Ten Plagues they realise that there are supernatural powers at work. Moshe outwits the Egyptian magicians and performs plagues they cannot reproduce. Even they admit that this is the "finger of G-d" at work. Moshe, in the name of G-d, constantly gives a warning followed by a plague. After the Ten Plagues and the Exodus, and especially after the splitting of the sea, the Torah attests to the fact that the people "believed in G–d and in Moshe His servant."

However, there would be one problem. The Jews had been told by a creature of flesh and blood that G–d had sent him with a message. There was still room for the sceptic – particularly in a later generation – to doubt. Thus, says *Rashba*, the stand at Sinai was necessary. Witnessed by an entire nation, G–d revealed Himself on Mount Sinai and gave the Ten Commandments. Each Jew experienced the same level of communication that Moshe received. Thereafter, the Jews were fully convinced that when Moshe transmitted the word of G–d it was truly Divine in origin.

It must be mentioned that the Children of Israel at that time were not uneducated slaves who could easily be fooled. Among them were great sages, priests, architects and builders, professionals who built pyramids and other structures – wonders of the world – whose architecture still baffles modern builders. They were a knowledgeable generation – and certainly argumentative and stiff necked as was displayed on many occasions. If part of the nation had "dreamt up" a story it would certainly have been rejected by the others.

The Exodus and revelation at Sinai remain undisputed historical facts. As previously mentioned, witnesses are the greatest proof in a court of law – how much more so, the eye witness account of an entire nation! That is certainly a most scientific proof of the existence of G–d. Although we cannot see Him – like the blind man who can't see colour – our ancestors witnessed this revelation and transmitted the fact as both an oral and a written tradition. It may be for this reason that in the first commandment G–d says, "I am the L–rd your G–d who brought you forth from the land of Egypt." The creation of the world is a much more complex and amazing phenomenon than the Exodus from Egypt, so why didn't G–d say, "I am the L–rd your G–d who created heaven and earth"? One possible answer is that scientists today still question the origin of the cosmos and some ignore the G–d issue. When G–d communicated with the Jews, he made the communication very personal. "I am the G–d you have witnessed taking you out of Egypt, and who now is talking to you." The people did not need any philosophical proofs. Their own eyes saw and their own ears heard. They were witnesses to the stand at Sinai. That is the greatest proof!

The best known prayer in Judaism is the *Shema*. In a *Sefer Torah* or *Mezuzah* the letter *Ayin* (ע) of the word *Shema* and the letter *Dalet* (ד) of the word *Echad* are written in large bold letters. Together they spell the Hebrew word *Ed* (עד) which means a witness. Whenever a Jew recites the *Shema* he bears witness to the existence of one G–d, an existence experienced by our forefathers and passed on to us through an unbroken line of tradition.

Philosophical proofs

In addition to the traditional proof we may now go on to look at other philosophical proofs. Many proofs have been cited and we shall limit ourselves in this chapter to the better known and most frequently quoted ones.

1. The classic work *Chovot Halevovot* (1:6) quotes a beautiful parable. Once a rabbi entered a king's palace and was granted an audience with the king. The king asked him the question, "how do you know of the existence of the Creator?" The rabbi respectfully asked the king to leave the room for a short while. On the table was a quill, an inkwell and some paper. While the king was out of the room, the rabbi wrote a beautiful poem on the paper. When the king returned he noticed the poem and was amazed at its poetic style. The ink was still wet and the king praised the rabbi for writing such a beautiful poem. The rabbi replied that he had not written the poem, rather, he had taken the inkwell, poured it onto the paper and the letters had formed themselves. The king ridiculed such a suggestion saying that it was impossible for the ink to arrange itself into a single letter, let alone a word, let alone a sentence, and certainly not into a beautiful poem! The rabbi replied, "there is your answer. If the ink in an inkwell cannot form a poem without the hand of a poet, then certainly the world, which is infinitely more complex than the poem,

could not possibly form itself without the hand of a Master Creator!"

A similar fictional story – though more contemporary – is told about the Americans, Russians and Chinese who got together and decided to send a manned space ship to Mars. After spending billions of dollars, roubles and yen, and after years of preparation, a space ship finally blasts off heading for Mars. A while later an astronaut takes a small step for man but a large step for mankind and steps out onto the Martian surface. The cameras beam his every move back to earth. Suddenly, after taking a few steps, the world is stunned by the sight of a can of Coca Cola lying on a nearby rock. The astronaut picks up the can, sees it's the real thing, for written on the can are the words "Coke trademark – made in the USA". The Russians and Chinese are in uproar – the Americans had obviously deceived them and sent an earlier spaceship. The Americans deny this claim but are baffled by the appearance of the can of Coke. Finally, the press interviews a professor from Oxford University who explains the conundrum by suggesting that over billions and billions of years it is quite possible that, through evolution etc., a can of Coke was formed, even displaying the words "made in the USA"!

His comments are ridiculed. Even after billions of years the mathematical probability of these words forming by themselves is nil. How much more so the creation of this world which is amazingly complex?

Even today, scientists agree that they have fathomed only the tip of the iceberg of the complexity of the universe. How could it possibly have formed by itself without a master architect and designer?

A similar story is told of a man who entered a fully automated car factory and, after seeing an entire car being produced by a machine from beginning to end, came to the conclusion that cars make themselves! How ridiculous to think that such a factory was not designed by a master mechanic and engineer!

2. Rabbi Aryeh Kaplan writes (*Handbook of Jewish Thought* 1:1):

> The existence of a purposeful Creator is indicated by the fact that the inorganic universe contains every ingredient needed to make organic life possible. The world exists as an arena for life, and the probability that this is entirely due to chance is infinitesimally small. The essence of the argument is that mathematically the more complex an ordered structure, the less the probability of its structure being due to chance. The chemistry of life is by far the most complex process in our experience, and yet we find that the inorganic matter of the universe can support this process. Since there is only one type of matter in the universe, the chances of its having all the chemical and physical properties needed to support life are remotely small, unless we take into account a purposeful Creator.

3. The *Talmud* states that man is a microcosm. Without even looking at the cosmos we see from the wonders of the human body that this is the work of a Master Creator, for, even over billions of years, nothing as complex as this could just have appeared.

Let us take an example from the human eye. A baby's eyes, which begin to form in the embryo at nineteen days, will have more than twelve million screen points per square centimetre; the retina, or light sensitive portion of the eye, will have more than fifty billion such points. The composite picture the eyes record is homogeneous because these light sensitive points blend into a whole. Take a hand lens and examine any picture in a daily newspaper. You will find it made up of hundreds of points, each light or dark, which together make up the picture as you look at it from a greater distance. This is exactly what the eye does, only in much finer detail.

Where do these billions of cells in the nervous system come from? From the fertilised ovum, which is still dividing after one month to form the tissues and organs that the child requires. It has been estimated that all two billion of the specific nerve cells which make any individual educable are located in the outer covering of the brain, its cortex, and that these two billion cells could be stored in a thimble. Development continues in certain parts of the brain, even after birth. By the end of the first month of embryonic development, none of these parts of the brain, spinal cord, nerves or sense organs is completely formed, but the foundation for them all has been laid.

The development of the brain and the nervous system, and its rule of the integration of all the systems remains one of the most profound mysteries of embryology.

The eyes alone display such intelligent planning as almost to stupefy anyone studying them. In the embryonic stage, the eyes are formed on the sides of the head and are ready for connection to the optic nerves growing out independently from the brain. The forces that ensure this integration have so far not been discovered but they must be formidable indeed since more than one million optic nerve fibres must mesh with each eye.

Think for a moment about what is considered to be a feat of human engineering – the drilling of tunnels from both sides of the Alps that must somehow meet precisely and merge into one continuous highway. Yet any one of the thousands of things the foetus must do as part of the routine of development is far more wondrous. (*The Obvious Proof* – CIS p.59)

The same could be said of the wonder of the baby's first breath. After receiving oxygen for nine months through the umbilical cord, in a matter of moments the lungs miraculously open without any faults. Before the first breath the tubes were non-operative and yet a breath later all tubes are full systems go. This is truly phenomenal.

We have taken only two out of thousands of examples of the wonders of nature to demonstrate that these systems are so complicated it is almost impossible that they formed by themselves and were not designed by a Master Creator. No wonder the Kabbalists say that one may see the soul through the eyes, and King David writes in the Psalms that one must praise G–d for each breath.

This realisation is reinforced by the recent deciphering of the genome – the human DNA chain. The astounding amount of genetic information contained in these chains makes the mind boggle. Could these super complex chains just have made themselves?

Conclusion

We may conclude from the very existence of life and the complexity of the universe that it must have been designed and sustained by a Master Creator. It was our patriarch Abraham who, through such logical deduction, came to the monotheistic conclusion – the belief in one G–d; one unified force that creates a most diverse universe. Abraham converted half of civilisation in his days to this belief and he transmitted that belief to his offspring. Seven generations later his children stood as a nation at Sinai where they received the Torah directly from G–d. The undisputed historical fact of the Exodus from Egypt and the stand at Sinai, coupled with the necessity for a master designer and architect of the cosmos, "prove" the existence of G–d.

The historical proof

There is one final proof that we must examine. This is neither tradition, nor philosophy; rather, proof of the existence of G–d as the G–d of history. The Jewish people are called the "Chosen People". They were chosen by G–d to fulfil a specific purpose – adherence to Torah and *mitzvot*, thereby creating an abode for G–d in this world. An in-depth review of Jewish history will inevitably lead to faith in G–d as the Master of the World.

Rabbi Meir Simcha Sokolovsky writes in his book, *Prophecy and Providence – The Fulfilment of Torah Prophecies in the Course of Jewish History* (Feldheim Publications),

> The Torah calls upon us to keep past events in mind and to study them. A study of the past will necessarily lead to the conviction that the direction of history was carefully programmed in advance and that the events of world and Jewish history have unfolded in accordance with a preconceived plan. Obviously, both the plan and its execution must be the work of the Creator who dominates history and directs its course.

At great length, he demonstrates in his book how,

1. The history of the Jewish nation up to the present time has corresponded in full with all the prophecies of the Torah.
2. According to the laws of nature Jewish history should have taken a different course from the one it actually followed. One is led to conclude that only a Creator, who alone controls the forces in the universe, could have determined beforehand what the future would hold.
3. The events of Jewish history are truly remarkable and extraordinary. Aside from having been predicted in advance, they serve as intrinsic proof of the unique and supernatural guidance which Jewry has always enjoyed as G–d's Chosen People.

To do justice to the subject matter one must actually read the book. However we shall give here a brief review which will, hopefully, encourage the reader to study the subject in more depth.

Before we do so, by way of introduction, it is well worth citing the famous quote from Mark Twain, "Concerning the Jews",

> To conclude – If the statistics are right, the Jews constitute but one per cent of the human race. It suggests a nebulous dim puff of star dust lost in the blaze of the Milky Way. Properly the Jew ought hardly to be heard of; but he is heard of, has always been heard of. He is as

prominent on the planet as any other people, and his commercial importance is extravagantly out of proportion to the smallness of his bulk. His contributions to the world's list of great names in literature, science, art, music, finance, medicine, and abstruse learning are always way out of proportion to the weakness of his numbers. He has made a marvellous fight in this world, in all the ages; and has done it with his hands tied behind him. He could be vain of himself, and be excused for it. The Egyptian, the Babylonian, and the Persian rose, filled the planet with sound and splendour, then faded to dream-stuff and passed away; the Greek and the Roman followed, and made a vast noise, and they are gone; other peoples have sprung up and held their torch high for a time, but it burned out, and they all sit in twilight now, or have vanished. The Jew saw them all, beat them all, and is now what he always was, exhibiting no decadence, no infirmities of age, no weakening of his parts, no slowing of his energies, no dulling of his alert and aggressive mind. All things are mortal but the Jew; all other forces pass, but he remains. What is the secret of his immortality? (Harper's Magazine, June 1899)

One of the Principles of Jewish faith is that G–d grants prophesy to man. When a prophet foretells the future, and everything he predicts takes place with amazing accuracy, we can be sure that this was the word of G–d. Nowhere else is this so remarkably demonstrated than in the Five Books of Moses. There are three passages in particular in which Moshe tells the Children of Israel what will happen to them in the future. In *Prophecy and Providence*, Rabbi Sokolovsky shows at great length how each and every prophecy was accurate and how it took place in the course of Jewish history. In this chapter we shall seek to précis his thesis.

Imagine if you were a reporter following the story of the Exodus of Jews from Egypt. You had been on site in Egypt witnessing the Ten Plagues and the splitting of the sea. You had travelled with the people throughout the forty years in the wilderness and you were now about to enter the Promised Land. You were granted an audience with Moshe – a press conference – in which Moshe, before he dies, is going to share his last will and testament with the world. You are expecting that Moshe will bless his people with good fortune, wishing them well on their entry and conquest of the land. You would expect him perhaps to admonish them, rather like a father who reminds his children to keep to the correct path. However, what happens at this press conference is somewhat different. Moshe proceeds to unravel a document in which – in the name of G–d – he prophesies exactly what will happen to this nation from the moment it enters into the land until the End of Days. You are shocked – how could Moshe possibly know in such detail of the following three thousand years of Jewish History, particularly when he unravels a tale so foreboding that one would consider his account a nightmarish tangle of falsehood that could not possibly occur in real life? How could a human being, standing on the plains of Moab, have such intimate insight into the future chronicles of this people? As a sceptic, you may have dismissed Moshe's predictions as fantasy.

However, standing today with the advantage of hindsight you look back at that first press conference and see that Moshe is true and his Torah is true. Everything that Moshe said came to pass. How could that be?

There is only one answer and only one conclusion. Moshe was a true prophet and he received and transmitted the word of G–d. Only the Master Creator could know of this tale and only He could weave the fabric of history to make it happen. An honest review of Jewish history points inexorably to the existence of G–d.

One final point before we start briefly examining those prophecies. At its inception as a nation the Jewish People experienced the guidance of Divine Providence. Divine intervention in human affairs was manifest and tangible. The whole nation clearly saw that there was a G–d in Israel. But, when the Jews began to stray from the ways of Torah, the Divine guidance of their fate changed into a different mode; it became hidden and covert – as the Torah tells us (Deuteronomy 31:17),

"And My wrath will be aroused against them on that day and I shall abandon them and conceal My face from them." When "that day" arrived the miraculous aspect of G–d's overt intervention in our history ceased, to be replaced by a covert intervention in man's destiny. This covert Providence leaves room for error and doubt, for it sometimes makes it appear as if, G–d forbid, He has abandoned His people.

Thus there began the two oscillating modes of G–d's manifestation. Sometimes His presence would be manifest and at other times concealed. This is, in fact, one of the most striking points of the Jewish calendar and yearly cycle. On *Pesach*, *Shavuot* and *Sukkot* we celebrate the fact that G–d delivered us from Egypt, gave us the Torah, and granted us Divine protection with the clouds of Glory. On *Chanukah* we celebrate the victory over the Greeks and light the *Menorah* to symbolise the spiritual victory over the assimilative forces of Hellenism. On *Purim*, we celebrate the frustrating of Haman's "Final Solution".

On all these days G–d's presence is clear. And yet on *Tisha B'Av* we weep and mourn the destruction of the Temples. On the other national fast days we lament the events which led to that destruction and other catastrophes of Jewish history. In this generation we are all still numbed by the graveyard of Jewish history, the Holocaust. At these times, G–d's presence was covert.

Yet the Jew celebrates and mourns simultaneously. He knows that his destiny stands far beyond the rules of nature and that the trials and tribulations of covert Providence are not merely due to chance, but rather to a meticulous realisation of G–d's premeditated and pre-calculated will. It is this very faith that allows the Jew to surf the waves of anti-semitism and mock our enemies. The Jew knows that he is eternal – he knows his secret of immortality. G–d has promised him (Jeremiah 5:18), "Even in those devastating days, says G–d, I will not make a full finish of you", and (Leviticus 26:44), "I will not reject them, neither will I abhor them, to destroy them utterly."

Let us now have a closer look at those prophecies. In two passages of the Torah, Moshe gives us a *Tochachah* (an admonition) Leviticus Ch.26 and Deuteronomy Ch.28. Nachmanides, in his commentary on the Bible, explains that these two passages were both fulfilled consecutively. Leviticus Ch.26 by the destruction of the first Temple and Deuteronomy Ch.28 by the destruction of the second Temple and the following arduous exile. A third passage in Deuteronomy Ch.30 speaks of the eventual repentance and redemption of the Jewish People.

Leviticus Ch.26
"And I will scatter you among the nations." – the first exile to Babylon.

"And I will bring the land into desolation." – the ruination of the Land of Israel.

"And I will bring your sanctuaries into desolation." – the destruction of the First Temple.

"And I will not smell the savour of your sweet odours." – the cessation of sacrifice in the first Temple.

"Then shall the land be paid her Sabbaths." – the duration of the first exile – 70 years – was commensurate with the number of Sabbatical years, which were not previously correctly observed.

"And you shall eat the flesh of your sons and the flesh of your daughters." – a prophecy fulfilled, as described by Jeremiah in the book of Lamentations (2:20), at the destruction of the first Temple.

One can ask, How was it possible for Moshe to know that, over eight hundred years after the Jews entered the Land of Israel under Joshua, the Babylonians would come and destroy the first Temple and exile the people for 70 years? How did he know about the cessation of offerings and the eating of the flesh? Only cognitive dissonance will allow the sceptic to deny that this was prophecy from the true G–d; the living G–d who creates, sustains and directs the course of the world.

Deuteronomy Ch.28

"And you shall be plucked off the land." – the second exile.

"Your sons and daughters shall be given unto another

nation ... and you shall serve your enemy ... in famine and thirst." – before the exile.

"The Lord will bring upon you a nation from afar, from the end of the earth." – a reference to Rome.

"... who will swoop down like an eagle." – a reference to the Roman legions whose standard bearers carried the sign of an eagle.

"And it will lay siege to all your gates, until your high and fortified walls ... are toppled." – the land is conquered, there is siege, and the walls fall.

"The stranger that is in your midst shall mount up above you higher and higher." – a reference to Herod.

"You shall betroth a wife, and another man shall lie with her." – a Roman decree.

"And G–d shall scatter you among all the peoples from one end of the earth to the other end of the earth." – the Jew is exiled to all four corners of the earth.

"And among these nations you shall have no repose, and there shall be no rest for the sole of your foot ... and you shall fear night and day." – the situation of Jews in exile.

"Your life shall hang in doubt before you." – no financial security.

"And as for them who are left of you, I will send a faintness into their hearts ... and you shall have no power to stand before your enemies." – the Jews are easily subdued.

"Each day's curse will surpass that of the day before." – events will happen so rapidly, the Jew will hardly be able

to recover from one incident before another calamity befalls him.

"You will be beset by illnesses and plagues not even mentioned in the Torah." – the many sufferings of exile.

"You shall serve gods ... wood and stone there." – a reference to the fact that, throughout their long exile, the Jew will be subjected to the god of wood – the cross – burnt at the stake with forced conversions; and to the god of stone of Mecca and Medina.

"I will draw out the sword after you ... and you shall perish among the nations and the land of your enemies will devour you." (see Leviticus 26:33,38) – decrees of forced conversion and pogroms.

"And you shall be left few in number among the nations whither G–d shall lead you away." – in fact it is quite amazing that, particularly during the Dark Ages, the Jew did not disappear totally.

"And you shall become an astonishment." – the Jews will become a topic of discussion for all.

"... a proverb and a byword." – the wandering Jew shall be the symbol of suffering and persecution.

"And they shall be upon you for a sign and for a wonder." – the badges we were often forced to wear identified us as the Jew.

In graphic detail Moshe prophesies the destruction of the second Temple and the following exile with amazing accuracy. He was talking about events that took place

1,500 years after he passed on. How could he possibly have known?

And yet the Jew still survives – and thrives.

"For I am G–d, I do not change, therefore you sons of Jacob are not consumed." (Malachi 3:6) – the eternity of the Jewish people.

"Only if the sun, moon and stars disappear, the seed of Israel shall also cease from being a nation." (Jeremiah 31:35)

Amidst great persecution, suffering and exile, Torah study flourished. There were always Talmudic academies producing Torah scholars who carried the baton of Torah learning and transmitted it to the next generation. This fulfils the prophecy, *"For it, the Torah shall not be forgotten from the mouth of their seed."* (Isaiah 59:20-21)

Throughout, the Jew kept *Shabbat*.

"The Shabbat *will be an everlasting covenant between G–d and Israel."* (Numbers 31:16)

"It is a sign between Me and the children of Israel." (*Ibid.*)

Isn't it fascinating that, when the other two main religions picked a day for their day of rest, one picked Sunday and the other Friday, but *Shabbat* remained the day of rest for the Jew? Was this not prophesied?

Most enlightening are the prophecies concerning the Land of Israel during the time when its people would be in exile:

"And your enemies that dwell in the Land of Israel shall be desolate in it." (Leviticus 26:32) The land belongs to us even when we are in exile. In our prayers we say, "because of our sins we were exiled from *our* land." Isn't it fascinating that, before the destruction of the Temples, the land was populous and fertile, and, after the destruction, it became a desolate land, a land of swamps? Mark Twain on a visit to the land expressed his surprise – could it be said that this is the Promised Land, a land flowing with milk and honey? The greatest number of people that inhabited the land from the time of the second exile until the turn of the twentieth century was 300,000 – in the times of the Turks – and even then the population dwindled due to earthquakes. Today, after the return of many Jews to the land, its population numbers in the millions. What was swamp has been reclaimed and is again green pasture. It was a land that was awaiting the return of its people.

Quite amazingly the only remaining wall of the second Temple, the *Kotel Maaravi* – the Western Wall – remained standing and was never destroyed. The rabbis stated that the Divine Presence never moved from the Wall.

And the story is not over yet. There is a passage in Deuteronomy Ch.30 that describes the full return and redemption of the Jewish nation.

It will be that when all these things come upon you – the

blessing and the curse that I have presented before you – then you will take it to your heart among all the nations where the Lord your G–d has dispersed you; and you will return unto the Lord your G–d, and listen to his voice, according to everything that I command you today, you and your children, with all your heart and all your soul. Then, the Lord your G–d will bring back your captivity, and have mercy upon you, and He will gather you in from all the peoples to which the Lord your G–d has scattered you. If your dispersed will be at the ends of the heaven, from there, the Lord your G–d will gather you in, and from there He will take you. The Lord your G–d will bring you to the land that your forefathers possessed and you shall possess it; He will do good to you and make you more numerous than your forefathers. The Lord your G–d will circumcise your heart and the heart of your offspring, to love the Lord your G–d, with all your heart and with all your soul, that you may live.

The Lord your G–d will place all these curses upon your enemies and those who hate you, who pursued you. You shall return and listen to the voice of G–d, and perform all His commandments that I command you today. G–d will make you abundant in all your handiwork – in the fruit of your womb, the fruit of your animals, and the fruit of your land – for good, when the Lord will return to rejoice over you for good, as He rejoiced over your forefathers, when you listen to the voice of the Lord your

G–d, to observe His commandments, and His decrees, that are written in this Book of the Torah, when you shall return to the Lord your G–d, with all your heart and all your soul.

For this commandment that I command you today – it is not hidden from you and it is not distant. It is not in the heaven, to say, "who can ascend to the heaven for us and take it for us, so that we can listen to it and perform it?" Nor is it across the sea for you to say, "who can cross to the other side of the sea for us and take it for us, so that we can listen to it and perform it?" Rather, the matter is very near to you – in your mouth and your heart to perform it.

See – I have placed before you today the life and the good, and the death and the evil, that which I command you today, to love the Lord your G–d, to walk in his ways, to observe His commandments, His decrees and His ordinances; then you will live and you will multiply, and the Lord your G–d will bless you in the land to which you come to possess it. But if your heart will stray and you will not listen, and you are led astray, and you prostrate yourself to strange gods and serve them, I tell you today that you will surely be lost; you will not lengthen your days upon the land that you cross the Jordan to come there, to possess it. I call heaven and earth today to bear witness against you; I have placed life and death before you, blessing and curse; AND YOU SHALL CHOOSE LIFE, so that you will live, you and your offspring – to love the Lord your G–d, to listen to His voice and to cleave to Him, for He is your life and the length of your days, to dwell upon the land that the Lord swore to your forefathers, to Abraham, to Isaac and to Jacob, to give them.

The *Talmud* is full of amazing predictions that will take place at the End of Days. These are now fully documented for the English reader. We refer you to the book *Mashiach* by Rabbi J.I.Schochet. See also Chapter 12 below.

Summary

In this chapter we have proved the existence of G–d
1. through witnessing the revelation of G–d at Sinai,
2. by philosophical proof,
3. with a brief study of the fulfilment of Biblical prophecies.

The *Talmud* refers to Jews as "Believers, children of Believers". It is almost as if belief in G–d is hereditary. In truth, however, innate belief stems from the very core of the Jewish soul. Job describes the soul as a "part of the Divine". The simple faith of a Jew comes from that which he feels the very source of his soul – his very essence. That essence may often become oblique through the insensitivities and indulgences of the body.

However, the quintessential point remains forever intact and, on those very special occasions when the soul shines forth, the Jew feels his true source, his very essence.

2

What is Life's Purpose?

We all wish to live a meaningful life. But why are we living? What are we doing in this world?

To find the answer to this central question we must look in the very book of life itself – the Torah, which is called *Torat Chaim* (a living Torah). The word "Torah" means "instruction" or "guidance", for the Torah is our guide in life. The Torah makes us constantly aware of our duties in life; it gives us a true definition of our purpose, and it shows us the ways and means of attaining this goal.

The creation of man

The Torah begins with Genesis. When Adam was created the Creator immediately apprised him of his powers and told him that his purpose in life would be to, "Replenish the earth, and conquer it; and have dominion over the fish of the sea, and over the fowl of the air, and over every living thing that moves upon the earth." (Genesis 1:18)

Man was given the power to conquer the whole world and to rule over it, on land, sea and in the air, and he was enjoined to do so; this was his task.

How was this "world conquest" to be attained and what is the purpose and true meaning of it?

Our Sages teach that when G–d created Adam, his soul – his Divine image – permeated and irradiated his whole being, by virtue of which he became ruler over the entire creation. All the creatures gathered to serve him and to crown him as their creator. But Adam, pointing out their error, said to them, "Let us all come and worship G–d our Maker!"

The "world conquest", given to man as his task and mission in life, was to elevate and refine the whole of nature, including the beasts and animals, to the service of true humanity; humanity permeated and illuminated by the Divine Image – by the soul, which is veritably a part of G–d above – so that the whole of creation will realise that G–d is our Maker.

Needless to say, before a man sets out to conquer the world he must first conquer himself and his own ego through the subjugation of the "earthly" and "beastly" in his own nature. This is attained through actions which accord with the directives of the Torah – the practical guide to everyday living – so that the material becomes permeated and illuminated with the light of the One G–d, our G–d.

G–d created one man and upon this single person on earth He imposed this duty and task. Herein lies the profound yet clear directive, namely, that one man – each and every person – is potentially capable of "conquering the world". If a person does not fulfil his task and does not utilise his inestimable Divine powers it is not merely a personal loss and failure but something that affects the destiny of the whole world.

One person can change the world

One of the main distinguishing features in the creation of man is that man was created as a single being, unlike other species which were created in large numbers.

This indicates emphatically that one single individual has the capacity to bring the whole of creation to fulfilment, as was the case with the first man, Adam. As mentioned above, no sooner was Adam created than he called upon and rallied all creatures in the world to recognise the sovereignty of the Creator with the cry, "Come, let us prostrate ourselves, let us bow down and kneel before G–d our Maker!" For it is only through "prostration" – self-abnegation – that a created being can attach itself to, and be united with, the Creator and thus attain fulfilment of the highest order.

The Rabbis teach us that Adam was the prototype and example for each and every individual to follow. "For this reason was man created single, in order to teach you that 'one person is equivalent to an entire world' ". This means that every Jew, indeed, every human being, regardless of time and place and personal status, has the fullest capacity (and also the duty) to rise and attain the highest degree of fulfilment, and accomplish the same for creation as a whole.

Rosh Hashanah – the birthday of man

This idea is underlined by the fact that the Jewish New Year – *Rosh Hashanah* – celebrates the birthday of man, which took place on the sixth day of creation.

In the liturgy of *Rosh Hashanah* we find that it is called the "day of the beginning of Your works" (text of prayer for *Rosh Hashanah*). Why is it the "beginning of Your works" when, in fact, *Rosh Hashanah* corresponds to the sixth day of the creation?

The answer is given by the Rabbis: Inasmuch as man is the ultimate purpose and *raison d'être* of all domains of the universe and since, with the creation of man, the whole of creation was completed and fulfilled, man, in effect, embodies the entire creation as if, before him, nothing was created.

Nevertheless, the question must be asked, How can this be true when there is a great world besides man, an impressive and noteworthy world, as it says in the Psalms, "How manifold are your works O G–d", and "How great are your works O G–d"? Moreover, considering the whole of creation, we find that the "speaking genus" – man – is numerically much less than the order of animals, and still less than the order of plants, and least in comparison to inorganic matter (earth, minerals etc.).

The answer – and this, indeed, is one of the basic teachings of *Rosh Hashanah* in regard to the entire creation – is as follows:

The order in the scale of all created things where inorganic substances exceed plants, and plants outnumber animals, and man is least of all, is based on consideration of quantity. However, when quality is considered, the order is reversed: inorganic matter, which has no signs of life and locomotion, is at the bottom of the scale; above it is the world of plants, endowed with growth but lacking the vitality and movement of animals; higher still is the animal kingdom which, since animals do not possess human intellect, is inferior to man – the highest of all creatures. For, although an animal has an intellect of its own, the animal intellect is not an end in itself but an instinct, whose function is to serve the natural needs of the animal. However, the human intellect – provided the person conducts himself as a human being and not as an animal – is mainly an end in itself. Furthermore, the human intellect attains its goal and fulfilment, not when it serves as an instrument for the gratification of physical needs, as in the case of animals, but, on the contrary, when all such natural functions as eating, drinking and the like, become servants of the intellect, in order that the person should be able to rise ever higher in intellectual and spiritual pursuits.

Yet this is not quite the true fulfilment of the human being. True fulfilment is achieved when the intellect leads him to the realisation that there is something higher than intellect, so that the intellect surrenders itself completely to that ideal.

To put it more clearly, human fulfilment is attained when intellect recognises that man, and with him the entire creation, must strive for and achieve acknowledgement of, and attachment to, G–d, the Creator of the Universe and Master of everything in it.

This concept directly relates to, and must permeate, our daily life as evidenced also by the fact that the Psalm beginning with, "G–d reigns, He robed Himself in majesty", has been instituted as the "Daily Psalm" for the sixth day of every week of the year. This is what Adam, the first man, accomplished when he acknowledged the sovereignty of the Creator, elevating himself and all creation to a level of recognising G–d.

The general lesson to be inferred from all this is as follows: Reflecting upon himself, a person will see that most of his life and most of his efforts are taken up with things which, at first glance, are material and mundane, such as eating, drinking, sleeping and the

What is Life's Purpose?

like. It is also evident that there is a greater number of "men of the world" than "men of the spirit". In general, one sees most people immersed largely in material pursuits. Hence, one may erroneously think that perhaps the material and physical aspects of life are the most important in the world.

Rosh Hashanah teaches us that the opposite is true. To be sure, it took five days and part of the sixth to create all sorts of creatures. Yet it was man, a very small part of creation in time and space, who was the essence and purpose of the entire creation. And in man, too, the essential thing is not the body, which is "dust from the earth", but the soul, the living spirit which G–d "breathed into his nostrils"; a soul which is "truly part of G–dliness Above." Only after man was created with the Divine spark within him did the entire creation become worthy and complete. Thus man can justly be described as the "beginning" of creation in all its domains, and *Rosh Hashanah*, the birthday of man, as "the day of the beginning of Your works."

The power of the righteous

Yet immediately after the creation the Biblical narrative continues with the temptation of the forbidden fruit, Adam's sin and subsequent exile from the Garden of Eden. The snake, synonymous with the evil inclination, persuades man to disregard the mission of his soul in return for momentary pleasure. Adam plunges mankind into a constant struggle between his good and evil inclinations.

The Sages describe what happened in the following way: At the time of creation the *Shechinah* – Divine Presence – rested on earth. After the sin of Adam the *Shechinah* removed itself from the earth to the first firmament (the Sages speak of the existence of seven firmaments i.e. spiritual levels), and after the sins of Cain and Abel, and the subsequent generation of Enosh, the *Shechinah* removed itself further to the second and third firmament etc., until the *Shechinah* was removed, through the sins of subsequent generations, to the seventh firmament. It was the righteous Abraham who, through his Divine service, returned the *Shechinah* by one level to the sixth firmament. His son Isaac and grandson Jacob, and thereafter subsequent generations of righteous people, returned the *Shechinah* further, until Moshe, the seventh generation from Abraham, returned the Divine Presence to this earth, when he built the Tabernacle in the wilderness and the *Shechinah* rested there.

One of the great teachings of the Baal Shem Tov, the founder of the chassidic movement, is that of an ongoing creative process. Divine creative energy is constantly pulsating through the creation, bringing it into being *ex nihilo* every single second. If G–d were to stop creating the world, even for an instant, it would revert to null and void, as before the creation. When the Sages talk about "removal of the Divine Presence" they are not suggesting that G–d literally removed Himself from the world – otherwise the world would cease to exist. Rather they are suggesting that sin creates an insensitivity to that Divine Presence. G–dliness is no longer manifest and felt by the creation. It is almost as though G–d is in exile from His world. This was the result of generations of sin and it was only through the efforts of the righteous that the world was again sensitised to the Divine Presence and became a fitting abode for His presence.

A dwelling for G–d

It was Abraham who initiated the process of return, bringing the Divine Presence from the seventh to the sixth firmament. He accomplished this by establishing a guesthouse in Beer Sheba and giving wayfarers food and drink. After they had eaten Abraham would ask them to say Grace. The Torah tells us, "And Abraham called there in the name of G–d." The Sages comment, "do not read, 'and he called', but read, 'and he made call,'" i.e. he encouraged others to call. Maimonides states that Abraham had such a powerful influence in his time that he managed to convert a good part of known civilisation to belief in monotheism.

This task was continued by his sons, and the

patriarchal traditions and belief in monotheism were continued and upheld even after the descent of Jacob to Egypt and subsequent servitude and bondage. Although steeped and assimilated into Egyptian culture, the Children of Israel, and in particular the tribe of Levi, maintained their identity and beliefs.

G–d had promised Abraham that his descendants would serve a strange nation only for a certain time, after which they would be redeemed. When the time of redemption arrived G–d sent Moshe, a great-grandson of Levi, son of Jacob, to fulfil that task. Pharaoh, a self-proclaimed god, was systematically destroyed by the Ten Plagues. He and his magicians were forced to admit that the "finger of G–d" was at work. Finally the Jewish people left Egypt, a redemption from bondage which became the prototype for all future redemptions.

They witnessed further miracles – the splitting of the sea and the defeat of the Amalekites. Forty-nine days after leaving Egypt they stood at the foot of Mount Sinai where they heard the Ten Commandments from G–d Himself. G–d gave His Torah-instruction to the entire nation. Shortly after Sinai He instructed Moshe, "Make for Me a sanctuary so that I may dwell among them."

Moshe began the construction of the *Mishkan* – the Tabernacle; a portable structure that housed the Holy

Ark, which contained the tablets of stone and the scroll of the Law. The Tabernacle was to be the prototype for all future synagogues. When the Tabernacle was finally completed and erected, the Divine Presence rested upon it. The Sages tell us that the task was now complete and the Divine Presence had now returned to the world.

The construction of the Tabernacle exemplifies the purpose of creation which, in the words of the Midrash is that, "G–d desired to have an abode in the lowest of all worlds". The purpose of man is to take the creation and permeate it with G–dliness.

This idea was exemplified in the Tabernacle. When the Jews left Egypt they took with them great wealth which they subsequently donated for the materials necessary for the construction of the Tabernacle. Every aspect of the mineral, vegetable and animal kingdoms was represented in the Tabernacle. The walls were made of wooden boards covered with gold. The offerings brought in the Tabernacle represented the elevation of the animalistic dimension within man and its dedication to a higher purpose. Every aspect of the Tabernacle transformed the material into the spiritual. Thus the Tabernacle, which our sages say was a microcosm, or symbol, of the universe, reflected our very task in the world: that is, to take the material and transform and elevate it for a spiritual purpose. For example, eating in order to be healthy to learn Torah and keep *mitzvot*, using animal hides for *mezuzot* and *tefillin*, and the like.

A dwelling within each person
Within the wording, "Make for Me a sanctuary, so that I may dwell among *them*", lies a deeper meaning. Grammatically it should have stated, "so that I may dwell in it" yet it states, "so that I may dwell among them." The Sages point out that the construction of the Tabernacle is a pointer for each and every person to make a dwelling place for the Divine Presence within themselves.

As mentioned previously, every person is infused with a Divine Soul. It is the task of the soul to make a *Mishkan* out of the body in which it resides by elevating all bodily functions to a Divine purpose.

In short, this means being able to connect every bodily function with G–d – and this is precisely the purpose of Torah and *mitzvot*. In the Torah, G–d instructs us how to connect every sphere of operation and function with G–d. For example, in terms of time, "six days you shall work and the seventh day you shall rest." The function of *Shabbat* is to allow a person to withdraw from the mundane and focus on the spiritual for one day a week. This, in turn, creates a new perspective on the week to come. By simply dedicating one day a week to study and prayer, one elevates the entire week.

What is Life's Purpose?

The laws of *Kashrut* connect a Jew in his eating habits and the laws of *Taharat Hamishpachah* elevate intimacy. And so it is with all the *mitzvot*.

The Sages tell us that a human being is made of 248 limbs and 365 sinews. These correspond to the 248 positive commandments and the 365 negative commandments of the Torah. The word *mitzvah* in Aramaic means "a connection". Thus, there are 613 ways of connecting with G–d. Man has the ability to connect his entire being with G–d. Upon achieving this task he creates an abode for G–d in this world, hence fulfilling the purpose of creation.

The worlds of the spiritual and the material are not in conflict. The ultimate purpose is that they be fused and the material permeated with the spiritual. The core of all *mitzvah* performance is to take the material creation and utilise it for a Divine purpose. This achieves a wonderful harmony both in the individual and in the world at large. This theme is not relegated to the synagogue or moments of religious practice. Rather it encompasses all times and places; wherever and whenever a person operates he is able to utilise the task at hand for its correct, Divine, purpose.

The rewards of the World to Come

The *Talmud* is replete with references to the World to Come. Maimonides describes it as a "world of souls", a spiritual plane to which the soul returns after its sojourn in this world. The soul is to give an account of its lifetime and, subsequently, its merits and demerits are carefully weighed on the Divine scales. It is then rewarded for its good deeds and Torah learning. The reward takes the form of a revelation of G–d's glory, "basking in the Divine light". It may be necessary for the soul to be cleansed from its indulgences and iniquities and so it is sent to *Gehinom*, a spiritual purification depot, after which it ascends to Heaven. The *Talmud* uses the terms "Garden of Eden" or the "Heavenly Academy" to describe various levels and stages of this heavenly reward.

In this sense this world is a mere "corridor before the World to Come", a temporary stepping stone where one may earn a place and seat in the World to Come. In fact the Sages state that, "better one hour of heavenly bliss in the World to Come than all the pleasures of this world" (Avot 4:17). One should not serve G–d merely to receive this reward yet G–d does not remain in debt and will reward a person for all his good deeds. To this aim there is an "eye watching, an ear listening and a hand writing" all of a person's actions in this world. An exact account is kept.

Yet, however great the rewards of the World to Come, they are not the ultimate purpose of creation. As stated above, the ultimate purpose is that G–d desired to have a dwelling in the lowest of all worlds, in *this* material and physical world. It is in this vein that the Sages state that, "better one hour of repentance and good deeds in this world than all of the World to Come". Although the revelations of the higher spiritual worlds are magnificent and a true reward for the soul's efforts, however, the ultimate desire of G–d is the good deeds and *mitzvot* of this world.

It is for this reason that there is no open mention of the World to Come in the scripture. The Torah is primarily concerned with life on this world. The soul exists before its descent and returns to the heavenly realm in the afterlife. It is a "descent for the purpose of ascent", the ascent being the fulfilment of the ultimate purpose in creation, the creation of a dwelling for G–d in this world.

King Solomon describes the soul as "the candle of G–d". For what purpose does G–d need a candle? Is there any place where it is dark before Him? The candle is needed for this world within which G–d has clothed His majesty. The soul illuminates the body and the world, enabling it to recognise the Creator, through fulfilment of the Torah and *mitzvot* in daily life.

Rabbi Shneur Zalman of Liadi, the founder of Chabad, used to say, "I do not want your Garden of Eden, I do not want your World to Come, I only want You, Yourself." He meant that although the spiritual bliss of the World to Come is great, G–d, Himself, is experienced only by fulfilling the ultimate purpose – with one hour of repentance and good deeds in this world.

A specific purpose

In addition, every soul has a specific purpose besides the general purpose of making an abode for G–d in this world. The Baal Shem Tov said that a soul, in addition to keeping the Torah and *mitzvot*, may descend to this world and live for 70 or 80 years just to do a favour for another in the material or the spiritual realms. How does one know one's own specific purpose? How does one know which favour is the purpose of one's soul's descent? The answer is that everything happens by Divine Providence and if a person is presented with a certain opportunity, this is certainly sent from Above and should be treated as if it is the purpose of one's soul's descent.

Our Sages stated, "everything is from the hands of heaven except the fear of Heaven." This means that whatever happens to a person is from Heaven. The particular time and place a person lives and his station in life, whether rich or poor etc., is decided from Above. A person's only contribution is "the fear of Heaven" – his reaction in any given situation. We are all presented with unique opportunities and challenges and it is our lot in life to utilise them for the Divine purpose.

What is Life's Purpose?

The soul's descent

Our Sages stated further, "each and every soul was in the presence of His Divine Majesty before coming down to this earth", and that, "the souls are hewn from under the Seat of Glory." These sayings emphasise the essential nature of the soul, its holiness and purity, and how it is completely divorced from anything material and physical; the soul itself, by its very nature, is not subject to any material desires or temptations, which arise only from the physical body and "animal soul".

Nevertheless, it was the Creator's Will that the soul – which is truly a "part" of the Divine, should descend into the coarse, physical world and be confined within, and united with, a physical body for scores of years in a state which is diametrically opposed to its spiritual nature. All this for the purpose of a Divine mission which the soul has to perform to purify and spiritualise the physical body and its related physical environment, making this world an abode for the Divine Presence. This can be done only through a life of Torah and *mitzvot*.

When the soul fulfils this mission all the transient pain and suffering connected with the soul's descent and life on this earth is not only justified, but infinitely outweighed, by the great reward and everlasting bliss which the soul enjoys thereafter.

A wasted opportunity

From the above one can easily appreciate the extent of the tragedy of disregarding the soul's mission on earth. For, in doing so, one causes the soul to descend to this world virtually in vain, for one has not achieved its purpose. Even where there are brief moments of religious activity in the study of Torah and the practice of the *mitzvot*, it is sad to contemplate how often such activity is tainted by the lack of real enthusiasm and inner joy, without recognition that these are the activities which justify existence.

Apart from missing the vital point through failure to take advantage of the opportunity to fulfil G–d's Will, thus forfeiting the eternal benefits to be derived therefrom, it is contrary to sound reason to choose that side of life which accentuates the enslavement and degradation of the soul while rejecting the good that is within it; namely, the great elevation that is to come from the soul's descent.

The proper thing to do is to make the most of the soul's sojourn on earth and a life which is permeated by the Torah and *mitzvot* makes this possible.

It is also abundantly clear that since G–d, who is the essence of goodness, compels the soul to descend from its sublime heights to the lowest depths for the purpose of the study of the Torah and the fulfilment of the *mitzvot*, it must mean that the value of Torah and *mitzvot* is very great.

Furthermore, the descent of the soul for the purpose of being elevated shows that there is no other way to obtain this objective except through the soul's descent to live on this earth. If there were an easier way G–d would not compel the soul to descend to this nether world. For only here, in what the kabbalists call the lowest world, can the soul attain its highest ascent, higher even than the angels, and, as our Sages say, "The righteous are superior to the (foremost) angels."

Serve G–d with joy

Reflecting on the greatness of the Torah and *mitzvot*, specifically pertaining to this life; reflecting also that the Torah and *mitzvot* are the only means to attain the soul's perfection and the fulfilment of the Divine purpose; one will experience a sense of real joy at one's fate and destiny, despite the many difficulties and handicaps, from within and without, which are inevitable on this earth. Only in this way can one live up to the injunction, "Serve G–d with joy", which the Baal Shem Tov made one of the foundations of his teachings, which is expounded at length in Chabad teachings and pointed out by Rabbi Shneur Zalman of Liadi in his monumental work, *Tanya* (Ch.26,31).

Ultimately, following such a path in life will lead to true happiness. Happiness – in the Jewish sense – may be defined as follows: when a person is doing what

G–d wants from him at any given moment then he may be truly happy. Therefore, if, at any given moment and situation, a person acts according to the directives of the Torah instruction, he is truly a happy and blessed person. This feeling transcends all worldly matters, for such a person understands that everything that happens in life is orchestrated by G–d.

Conclusion

It is obviously necessary to study Torah and be aware of how to fulfil its directives in one's daily life. Torah is Divine wisdom and there is no greater union with G–d than by the intellectual unity of study. Yet, "the deed is the main thing." The ultimate purpose of study is to lead to action – to *mitzvah* performance – in fulfilling the purpose of creation, the making of an abode for the Divine in this world.

Each and every *mitzvah* has a cosmic effect and reveals the presence of G–d. The full revelation of this effect will be apparent when *Mashiach* comes. In that era, man's entire pursuit will be to know G–d.

Jerusalem, the spiritual capital of the world is made up of two Hebrew words, *yirah* and *shalem*, meaning "perfect awe". The rebuilding of Jerusalem denotes the reconstruction in the world of that perfect state of awe and the full presence of G–d which was found in the Garden of Eden. Every individual *mitzvah* is a step in fulfilling that goal.

What is Life's Purpose?

We would do well to heed the advice of King Solomon, the wisest of all men, when he wrote at the end of the book of Ecclesiastes,

> Ultimately, all is known; fear G–d, and observe His commandments; for this is the whole purpose of man.

In the words of our Sages, "I was created for the sole purpose of serving my Maker."

3

The Chosen People: Chosen for What?

"You have chosen us from among the nations" (*Siddur*). The Jews are referred to as "the Chosen People". Many Jews themselves ask, "for which task have we been chosen?"

The answer to this question lies in the Torah passage (Exodus 19:3-6) in which G–d addresses Moshe immediately prior to His revelation at Sinai:

> Moshe ascended to G–d, and G–d called to him from the mountain, saying, "So shall you say to the House of Jacob, and relate to the children of Israel: 'You have seen what I did to Egypt, and that I have borne you on the wings of eagles and brought you to Me. And now, if you hearken well to Me and observe My covenant, you shall be to Me the most beloved treasure of all peoples, for Mine is the entire world. You shall be to me a kingdom of priests and a holy nation.' These are the words you shall speak to the Children of Israel."

These words encapsulate the reason G–d "chose" the Jews; namely, to be a "kingdom of priests and a holy nation".

THE CHOSEN PEOPLE: CHOSEN FOR WHAT?

The reference here to priests does not refer to the *Kohanim*, priests who are descendants of Aaron the High Priest, for clearly all Israel are not priests in that sense. Rather, the reference here is to the "priestly function".

The priest's function is to "bring" G–d to the people, and to elevate the people to be nearer to G–d. The purpose of the Jews is to bring G–d to the world and the world closer to G–d.

In our association with the outside world every one of us – man or woman – must fulfil priestly functions. The juxtaposition of a "kingdom of priests" and "a holy nation" indicates that through being holy and dedicated to Torah and *mitzvot* in our private lives we can be successful ambassadors to the outside world. Our impact on the outside world is intrinsically related to our dedication to Torah and *mitzvot*.

This "priestly function" was termed by the prophet Isaiah as a "light to the nations".

Wherever Jews find themselves, in the Diaspora or in the Land of Israel, even a single Jew in a remote corner of the earth, it behoves every Jew, and every Jewish community to remember that they are part of, and representatives of, the entire Jewish people, and hence mandated with this task. Even when Jews are in *Galut* (exile) it is only the Jewish body that is in exile. The Jewish soul is never exiled and is free from any external subjugation. Consequently, while in exile, Jews must not ignore their task, nor underestimate their capacities, however limited their material powers may be.

The extent of one's duty is in direct proportion to one's station in life. It is all the greater in the case of an individual who occupies a position of some prominence which gives him an opportunity to exercise influence over others, especially youth. Such people must fully appreciate the privilege and responsibility which Divine Providence has vested in them to spread the light of the Torah and to fight darkness wherever and in whatever form it may rear its head.

Let no one think, "who am I, and what am I, to have such tremendous powers?" For we have seen – to our sorrow – what even a small quantity of matter can do in the way of destruction through the release of atomic energy. If such power is concealed in a small quantity of matter for destructiveness – in denial of the design and purpose of creation – how much greater is the creative power entrusted to every individual to work in harmony with the Divine purpose. In this case, one is given special abilities and opportunities by Divine Providence to attain the goal for which we have been created; the realisation of a world in which, "Each creature shall recognise that You created him, and every breathing soul shall declare, 'G–d, the G–d of Israel, is King, and His reign is supreme over all' " (*Rosh Hashanah* prayers).

Not by might or power but with spirit
The Jewish people have been given the directive, "Not by might nor by power, but by My spirit, says G–d." To the Jewish people and Jewish community (even to the Jew as an individual), special Divine capacities have been given to carry out their task in the fullest measure. For, where Jews are concerned, their physical powers are linked with, and subordinated to, their spiritual powers, which are infinite.

An historic example of this is found in the time of King Solomon when the Jewish people stood out among the nations of the world by virtue of having attained the highest degree of its perfection. Our Sages, referring to that state, describe it as being like "the moon in its fullness", for, as is well known, the Jewish people are likened to the moon, and they "reckon" their times (calendar months) by the moon. One of the explanations of this is that just as the moon goes through periodic changes in its appearance, according to its position *vis-à-vis* the sun, whose light it reflects, so the Jewish people go through changes according to the measure of their reflecting the light of G–d, of Whom it is written, "For G–d *Elokim* is sun and shield."

This perfection in the time of King Solomon (notwithstanding the fact that, even then, Jews constituted numerically and physically "the fewest of all the nations") expressed itself in quite a distinctive form in the relations between the Jewish people and the other nations of the world. The reputation of King Solomon's wisdom aroused a strong desire among kings and leaders to come and see his conduct and learn from his wisdom – the wisdom he had prayed for and received from G–d; permeated with G–dliness.

And when they came they also saw how, under his leadership, there lived a people, even in its material life, "with security, every man under his vine and under his fig-tree", in a land where, "the eyes of G–d, your G–d, are constantly on it, from the beginning of the year to the end of the year." And this is what brought peace between the Jews and the nations all around.

Thus it was clearly demonstrated that when Jews live in accord with Torah, true peace is attained, and they serve as a guiding light for the nations – "the nations will go by your light" – the light of Torah and *mitzvot*.

The task of the Jew and of the Jewish community is not limited to the time when they are in a state of a "full moon", but also when in exile, "spread and dispersed among the nations."

For even then they are one people, whose laws are different from those of all other nations, a fact that is known and acknowledged by all nations of the world.

4

Why is Life so Difficult?

Judaism teaches us that G–d is Master of the universe, whose omnipotent power is not limited in time and space. Moreover, G–d is the source of goodness and He desires His human creatures to live a life based on justice, morality and, insofar as Jews are concerned, a life fully in accord with the Torah and *mitzvot*.

Why is it, therefore, that such a life is often burdened with difficulties; sometimes, even seemingly insurmountable obstacles?

This question is not only raised by sceptics, but even by those who believe in Divine Providence. In fact, the deeper the belief in G–d's benevolence, the deeper the difficulty to reconcile this anomaly.

Consider the following:

Should a person strive towards a state of life in which he can enjoy the maximum pleasure with the minimum effort, or should he prefer a life of toil and maximum achievement, a life of much action and much accomplishment?

Needless to say, this is not an abstract question, for, in resolving it, the foundation is laid for the individual's concept of the pattern of his life, and how he will respond to what is happening both to and around him, even in matters not directly relating to him, and certainly in matters which directly affect his life.

On the basis of our faith and our Torah we are committed to the principle that the Creator and Master of the World – including the "small world", namely man – is the essence of goodness, and that it is the "nature of the Good to do good".

At first glance, it would therefore appear reasonable to suppose that the highest perfection is to be found in a state where the maximum pleasure – true pleasure – is obtainable without difficulty and without travail; for in such a state the "nature of the Good to do good" would be perceived in the fullest measure.

Yet the Torah, which is called *Torah Or* ("A Torah of light", showing things in their true essence) declares, "Man is born to toil". Even before his downfall, Adam was placed in the Garden of Eden with the assigned task "to till it and guard it"; only later did G–d tell him, "of all the trees of the garden you may eat."

To be sure, G–d could have established a world order in which morality and ethics would reign supreme with little or no effort on the part of man. The explanation for His not doing so, which resolves this apparent contradiction, is given in the Torah.

G–d desires that man should enjoy the good in its perfection although human nature is such that a person derives true pleasure only if he is a partner in its attainment, through his own exertion and travail; however, if he receives it entirely *gratis*, it is degrading to him as though he were receiving charity (bread of shame). Precisely because of this, the good in its perfection is enjoyed when a person earns it through hard work, and the harder the effort the sweeter the fruit of achievement.

Knowing that there is a Divine command to follow a certain path in life, a person is resolved to fulfil his Divine mission no matter what the difficulties may be. Indeed, he may regard the very obstacles which he encounters as a challenge to be faced unflinchingly and overcome. Far from being stymied by such obstacles, they may reinforce his determination and stimulate his effort to the maximum degree.

Coupled with this is the feeling of satisfaction, commensurate only with the amount of effort exerted in the struggle, which makes the fruits of victory so much more enjoyable.

You can do it

It is self-evident that the Creator, who knows the world and its creatures, would not give an order or command too difficult to carry out. If He has given specific commandments for each and every Jew, in his own unique circumstances, to fulfil, it is certain that He has first given us the capacity to fulfil them.

Some Jews are born with greater natural capacities, others with less, therefore the challenges and trials that G–d presents to each are in keeping with their strength. As our Sages say, "G–d does not deal despotically or arbitrarily with His creatures" and He does not expect the impossible. If a person is faced with great trials this, in itself, is proof that he has the capacity and strength to overcome them. Nothing stands in the way of the will and, given the proper effort, it is possible to overcome all difficulties.

The Amalekites

When the Israelites triumphantly marched out of Egypt on their way to Sinai, it seemed they were invincible, a nation surrounded by miracles; in one word, untouchable. And yet, brazenly, the Amalekites attacked them, an act we are commanded to remember.

Amalek, in the wider sense, represents all the obstacles and hindrances which a Jew encounters on his way to receive and observe the Torah and *mitzvot* with enthusiasm and joy in everyday life. Amalek represents apathy, indifference and depression. The command never to forget Amalek reminds us that Amalekites exist in every generation and in every day and age, and that we must not allow ourselves to be deterred or discouraged by them, wherever they appear.

Every Jew has been given the necessary powers to

overcome all such "Amalekites" and he is expected to use them in order to demonstrate to himself and others that nothing will deter him, nor dampen his fervour, to observe the Torah and *mitzvot* in accordance with G–d's Will. Once he recognises that any difficulty he encounters is really a test of his faith in G–d, and resolves firmly to meet the challenge, he will see that no Amalek of any kind is a match for the Divine powers of the Jewish soul. Indeed, far from being insurmountable obstructions, they turn out to be aids and catalysts for ever greater achievements. They have been instrumental in mobilising those inner powers which would have otherwise remained dormant.

They are our life
This leads to an even deeper insight.

The true and perfect way of fulfilling G–d's Will, which is embodied in the Torah and *mitzvot*, is not when it is prompted by a desire to discharge an obligation towards G–d and our fellowman. Neither is it the gratifying feeling of having contributed something towards the world at large. For so long as the Jew's compliance with the Will of G–d is externally motivated – however commendable such motivation is in itself – it is not yet quite complete. The perfect fulfilment of the Torah and *mitzvot* is achieved when such fulfilment is an integral part of one's life to the extent of being completely identified with oneself: that is to say when the Torah and *mitzvot* permeate a person's very essence and being, and become inseparable from him in his daily life.

This is the deeper meaning of the words which we declare daily in our prayer, "For they (the Torah and *mitzvot*) are our life" – meaning that, just as a person and his life are one, making him a living person, so are the Torah and *mitzvot* and the Jew, one and inseparable. Such real identification cannot be experienced if it is achieved with little effort. It becomes an integral part of one's life only when it entails extraordinary effort in striving for it, even to the extent of staking one's life in obtaining and holding it. Only something which is regarded as indispensable and integral to one's life can evoke one's innermost powers, and even self-sacrifice.

The ultimate purpose of Galut

The above provides an insight also into the meaning of the *Galut* (the exile and dispersion among the nations of the world), which is at the root of most, if not all, the difficulties and obstacles confronting the Jew in his desire to live his G–d given way of life.

To be sure, we recognise the *Galut* as a punishment and rectification for failure to live up to our obligations in the past as, indeed, we acknowledge in our prayers, "For our sins we were banished from our land." But punishment, according to our Torah, which is also called

Torat Chessed (a Torah of lovingkindness), must also essentially be *Chessed*.

G–d has ordained a certain group of people, the Jewish People, to carry out the difficult and challenging task of spreading, in every place, to the remotest corners of the world, the Unity of G–d – true monotheism – through living and spreading the light of Torah and *mitzvot*. This is a task which no other group was willing to undertake, or capable of carrying out. The greatest reward is the fulfilment of this destiny, or, as our Sages put it, "The reward of a *mitzvah* is the *mitzvah* itself." Thus, the ultimate purpose of the *Galut* is linked with our destiny to help bring humanity to a state of universal recognition of G–d.

A call to our generation

Paving the way to the gradual achievement of this destiny has always been the indomitable work of determined individuals and groups conscious of their responsibility. They dedicated themselves to the vital need of strengthening and spreading the Torah and *mitzvot* among all sections of our people.

In recent generations, more than ever before, the main emphasis has been on the need to bring the knowledge and practice of the Torah and *mitzvot* to all Jews, in the greatest number of locations – without waiting for them to seek it – in the hope that they will sooner or later realise the need of it themselves. The most effective way to accomplish this is, of course, through organised Torah-true education of the young; both the young in years and the "young" in knowledge.

The pattern has been set by the founders of *Chassidut* and of *Chassidut Chabad*, who exemplified this approach with dedication and selflessness. Before revealing himself and his way of life, the Baal Shem Tov was a *Melamed* – a teacher of small Jewish children. Similarly, Rabbi Shneur Zalman, the Alter Rebbe, founder of Chabad, who was a disciple of the Baal Shem Tov's disciple and successor, began his work by founding his well known three *Chadarim* (higher education institutions). This road has also been followed by his successors, the heads of *Chabad*, each in his own generation.

They personified an indomitable spirit and a disdain for any difficulties and obstacles in their work, making it plain for all to see that these are nothing but a challenge to be expected and to be overcome. By facing up to, and overcoming, all obstacles, they verified the truth of the basic tenets of our faith, namely that G–d's Providence extends to each and every one individually, and that, "He who is determined to purify himself and others, receives aid from On High".

It is a fact of common experience that when there is a firm will and unshakeable determination it soon becomes apparent that difficulties are often largely imaginary and, even when real, not insurmountable. The forces of good are cumulative and self-generating as our Sages indicated in their well-known dictum, "One *mitzvah* brings another in its train." If evil can be contagious, good is certainly much more so, and many who stand at the sidelines are inspired and willing to join in constructive and positive action provided the lead is given and the way is shown.

The challenge of our time is to spread the knowledge of the Torah and *mitzvot*, particularly through the education of our young, until each and every Jew attains the level of "Know the G–d of Your father and serve Him with a perfect heart", thus fulfilling the prophecy, "They all shall know Me, small and great, and the earth will be filled with the knowledge of G–d, as the waters cover the sea".

5

What is the Secret of Jewish Survival?

The story of Purim, as related in the Book of Esther, gives us a clear analysis of the "Jewish problem".

Being dispersed over 127 provinces and lands, their own still in ruins, the Jews undoubtedly differed from one another in custom, dress and language, according to the place of their dispersal, very much in the same way that Jews in different lands differ nowadays. Yet, though there were Jews who would conceal their Jewishness, Haman, the enemy of the Jews, recognised the essential qualities and characteristics of the Jews which made all of them, with or without their consent, into one people, namely, "their laws are different from those of any other people." (Esther 3:8)

Hence, in his wicked desire to annihilate the Jews, Haman seeks to destroy "all the Jews, young and old, children and women." Although there were in those days, too, Jews who adhered to the Torah and *mitzvot*, and Jews whose religious ties with their people were weak, or who sought to assimilate, none could escape the classification of belonging to that "lone people", and every one was included in Haman's cruel decree.

In all ages there were Hamans, yet we have outlived them, thank G‑d. Wherein lies the secret of our survival?

The answer will be evident from the following illustration. When a scientist seeks to ascertain the laws governing a certain phenomenon, or to discover the essential properties of a certain element in nature, he must undertake a series of experiments under the most varied conditions in order to discover those properties or laws which under all conditions are alike. No true scientific law can be deduced from a minimum number of experiments, or from experiments under similar or only slightly varied conditions, for the results as to what is essential, what is secondary or what is unimportant would then not be conclusive.

The same principle should be applied to our people. It is one of the oldest in the world, beginning its national history with the Revelation at Mount Sinai some 3,300 years ago. In the course of these long centuries our people has lived under extremely varied conditions, in different times and different places all over the world. If we wish to discover the essential elements making up the cause and very basis of the existence of our people and its unique strength, we must conclude that it is not its peculiar physical or intrinsic mental characteristics, nor its tongue, manners and customs (in a wider sense), nor even its racial purity (for there were times in the early history of our people, as well as during the Middle

Ages and even recent times, when whole ethnic groups and tribes have become proselytes and part of our people).

The only link which unites our dispersed and scattered people throughout its dispersion, regardless of time, is Torah and *mitzvot*, the Jewish way of life which has remained basically the same throughout the ages and in every place. The conclusion is clear and beyond doubt: It is Torah and *mitzvot* which has made our people indestructible in the face of massacres and pogroms aimed at our physical destruction, and in the face of ideological onslaughts of foreign cultures aimed at our spiritual destruction.

Purim teaches us the age-old lesson, which has been verified even most recently, to our sorrow, that no manner of assimilation, not even when it is extended over several generations, provides an escape from the Hamans and Hitlers; nor can any Jew sever his ties with his people by attempting such an escape.

On the contrary, our salvation and our existence depend precisely upon the fact that "their laws are different from those of any other people."

Purim reminds us that the strength of our people as a whole, and of each Jew and Jewess individually, lies in our close adherence to our ancient spiritual heritage which contains the secret of harmonious life and, hence, of a healthy and happy one. All other things in our spiritual and temporal life must be free from any contradiction to the basis and essence of our existence, and must be attuned accordingly in order to make for the utmost harmony, and to add to our physical and spiritual strength, which go hand-in-hand in Jewish life.

Assimilation is not the answer

In the human organism there are common functions in which all organs of the body participate in a joint effort; and there are specific functions pertaining to individual organs. In the latter case, the individual organ must make a special effort to fulfil its particular function while the common functions are carried out much more easily.

What would happen if a particular organ surrendered its individuality and its particular function, applying its energy solely towards the common functions?

At first glance it would seem to benefit thereby in saving much effort and in the ability to increase its share in the fulfilment of the common functions of the body. Yet, needless to say, the results would be disastrous, both for the individual organ and for the organism as a whole, for the individual organ would lose its identity and essence which are predicated precisely on its ability to perform a particular function. Failure to exercise this function would, moreover, lead to its atrophy and also, eventually, complete uselessness in the fulfilment of the common functions. As for the organism as a whole, its deprivation of the particular function and the eventual loss of the organ, would be injurious to the whole body, and even fatal, if the organ in question were a vital one.

This analogy can truly be applied to the individual in society, to a minority within a state, and to a nation within the community of nations. It is certainly true in our case, both on the national level as a people and in regard to every Jew individually.

The Jewish people, of whom it has been said long ago "for you are the fewest of all peoples" is a small minority among the nations of the world, and the individual Jew is a minority in his environment; even living in the midst of his own people, for there are places, sad to say, where the Jew living Jewishly, i.e. in accord with our holy Torah and the observance of its precepts in his daily life, is in the minority.

What is the specific function of our people and of the Jew as an individual?

It is, of course, easier to ascertain the individual function of any particular organ in the body than the function of a people in the community of nations. However, in the case of the Jewish people, which is unique in its extremely varied experiences and long history, the answer is not difficult to find. By a process of simple elimination, we can easily ascertain what factors have been essential to its existence and survival, and thus determine the essential character and function of our people.

An objective, unprejudiced survey of the long history

of our people will at once bring to light the fact that it was not material wealth, nor physical strength, that helped us to survive. Even during the most prosperous times under the united monarchy of King Solomon, the Jewish state and its people were materially insignificant in comparison with such contemporary world empires as Egypt, Assyria and Babylonia. That it was not statehood nor homeland is clear from the fact that, for most of the time, by far, our people possessed no independent state and has lived in the diaspora. That it was not the language is likewise clear from the fact that, even in Biblical times, Aramaic began to supplant the Holy Tongue as the spoken language; parts of the Scripture and almost all of our Babylonian *Talmud*, the Zohar, etc., are written in that language. In the days of Saadiah and Maimonides, Arabic was the spoken language of most Jews, while later it was Yiddish and other languages. Nor was it any common secular culture that preserved our people since that changed radically from one era to another.

The one and only common factor which has been present with Jews throughout the ages in all lands and under all circumstances is the Torah and its *mitzvot*, which Jews have observed tenaciously in their daily life.

To be sure, there arose occasionally dissident groups that attempted to break away from true Judaism, such as the idolatrous movements during the first Temple period, the Hellenists during the second, Alexandrian assimilationists, Karaites, etc., but they have disappeared. Such dissident groups uprooted themselves from their natural soil and, far from being constructive, became the worst enemies of the Jewish people and, thus, their persecutors.

Considered without prejudice, Torah and *mitzvot* must be recognised as the essential purpose and essential function of our people, whether for the individual Jew, or in relation to the Jewish people's role within humanity as a whole.

Hence the logical conclusion that the policy of imitating the other nations, far from helping to preserve the Jewish people, rather endangers its very existence, and, instead of gaining their favour, will only intensify their antagonism. In like manner, those Jews who court the favour of non-religious groups by concession and compromise in matters of Torah and *mitzvot* not only undermine their own existence and that of our people as a whole – for the Torah and *mitzvot* are our very life – but they defeat even their immediate aim, for such a policy can evoke only derision and contempt; and justifiably so, for a minor concession today leads to a major one tomorrow, and an evasion of duty towards G–d leads to an evasion of duty towards man, and who is to say where this downsliding will stop?

Earnest introspection will show that the essential factor of our existence and survival is our adherence to the Torah and the practice of its precepts. Let no one delude himself by taking the easier way out, nor be bribed by any temporary advantages and illusory gains.

The secret of our existence is in our being "a people that dwells alone" (Numbers 23:9), every one of us, man or woman, believing in the One G–d, leading a life according to the one Torah, which is eternal and unchangeable. Our "otherness", independence of thought and conduct are not our weakness but our strength. Only in this way can we fulfil the function imposed on us by the Creator, to be to G–d a "kingdom of priests and a holy nation", thereby being also a *segulah* (G–d's treasure) for all humanity.

The fifth son

The Festival of Passover is inaugurated by the central theme, "When your son will ask you", and the *Haggadah* is based on the commandment of the Torah, "Then you shall tell your son".

There are various ways of asking questions and formulating the answers depending upon whether the son belongs to the category of the "Wise", the "Wicked", the "Simple", or "The One Who Knows Not How to Ask".

While the "Four Sons" differ from one another in their reaction to the *Seder* Service they have one thing in common: they are all present at the *Seder* Service. Even the so-called "Wicked" son is there, taking an active, though rebellious, interest in what is going on in

Jewish life around him. This, at least, justifies the hope that some day even the "Wicked" son will become wise, and all Jewish children attending the *Seder* will become conscientious Torah and *mitzvot* observing Jews.

Unfortunately, there is, in our time of confusion and obscurity, another kind of Jewish child: the child who is conspicuous by his absence from the *Seder* Service; the one who has no interest whatsoever in Torah and *mitzvot*, laws and customs; who is not even aware of the *Pesach Seder*, of the Exodus from Egypt and the subsequent Revelation at Sinai.

This presents a grave challenge which should command our attention long before Passover and the *Seder* night, for no Jewish child should be forgotten and given up. We must make every effort to save that "lost" child and bring the absentee to the *Seder* table. Determined to do so, and driven by a deep sense of compassion and responsibility, we need have no fear of failure.

In order to remedy an undesirable situation of any kind it is necessary to attack the roots of the evil. The same is true in this case.

The regrettable truth is that the blame for the "lost generation" lies squarely on the shoulders of the parents of a bygone immigrant generation.

It was the result of an erroneous psychology and a misguided policy on the part of some immigrants arriving in a new and strange environment. Finding themselves a small minority and encountering certain difficulties, which are largely unavoidable in all cases of resettlement, some parents had the mistaken notion, which they injected also into their children, that the way to overcome these difficulties was to become quickly assimilated with the new environment by discarding the heritage of their forefathers and abandoning the Jewish way of life. Finding the ensuing process somewhat distasteful, as such a course is bound to be, and full of spiritual conflict, some parents resolved that their children be spared the conflict altogether. In order to justify their desertion and appease their injured conscience it was necessary for them to devise some rationale and they deluded themselves, and their children, by the claim that the the observance of the Torah and *mitzvot* did not fit in their new surroundings. They looked for, and therefore "found", faults with the true Jewish way of life while, in their non-Jewish environment, everything seemed to them only good and attractive.

By this attitude these parents hoped to assure their children's existence and survival in a new environment. But what kind of existence is it if everything spiritual and holy is traded for material things? What kind of survival is it if it means the sacrifice of the soul for the amenities of the body?

Moreover, in their retreat from *Yiddishkeit*, they turned what they thought was an "escape to freedom" into an escape to servitude, pathetically trying to imitate the non-Jewish environment, failing to see that such imitation, based on caricature and an inferiority complex, can only call forth mockery and derision, and can only offend the sensibilities of those whose respect and acceptance they are so desperately trying to win.

The same false approach to the minority problem, whereby the misguided minority seeks to ensure its existence by self-dissolution, (which essentially means suicide, or, at any rate, weakening) has dominated not only individuals, but unfortunately has been made the creed of certain groups thrown together by a set of circumstances. This gave rise to certain dissident movements on the Jewish scene which, either openly or covertly, sought to undermine the Divine Torah which gives our people its unique and distinctive character among the nations of the world. In truth, these movements, while differing from each other, have one underlying ideology in common, that of, "We will be as the nations, as the families of the countries, to serve wood and stone". (Ezekiel 20:32)

The dire consequence of this utterly false approach was that thousands upon thousands of Jews were removed from their fountain of life, from their fellow Jews and from their true faith. Deprived of spiritual life and content, there grew up children who no longer belong to the "Four Sons" of the *Haggadah*, not even to the category of the "Wicked" son.

Today, many Jews are the third or fourth generation of immigrants and are, halachically, in the category of a *Tinok Shenishbah* (a child abducted at an early age), meaning one who did not have the opportunity of a true Jewish education. Through assimilation and intermarriage they are in great danger of losing their Jewish identity. What can be done?

The way forward
The event of the Exodus from Egypt and the Festival of Passover are timely reminders, among other things, that the hope for survival, deliverance and freedom lies not in an attempt to imitate the environment but rather in unswerving loyalty to our traditions and true Jewish way of life.

Our ancestors in Egypt were a small minority and lived in the most difficult circumstances. Yet, as our Sages relate, they preserved their identity and, with pride and dignity, tenaciously clung to their way of life, traditions and distinct uniqueness; precisely in this way was their existence assured, as also their true deliverance from slavery, both physical and spiritual.

It is one of the vital tasks of our time to exert all possible effort to awaken in the young generation, and also in those who are advanced in years but still immature in deeper understanding, a fuller appreciation of the true Jewish values, a full and genuine Torah-true *Yiddishkeit*; not of that which goes under a false label of misrepresented, compromised, or watered-down "Judaism", whatever the trade-mark. Together with this appreciation will come the realisation that only true *Yiddishkeit* can guarantee the existence of the individual, of each and every Jew, at any time, in any place, and under any circumstance.

There is no room for hopelessness in Jewish life, and no Jew should ever be given up as a lost cause. Through the proper compassionate approach of loving a fellow Jew, even those of the lost generation can be brought back to the love of G–d (*Ahavat-HaShem*) and love of the Torah (*Ahavat-HaTorah*), and can not only be included in the community of the "Four Sons" but, in due course, be elevated to the rank of the "Wise" son.

6

Can One Be a Good Jew Without Being Religious?

Many people feel that life in accordance with Torah and *mitzvot* is restrictive, limiting the individual in personal creativity, particularly in the area of thinking and choosing for oneself. It is hard to reconcile such commitment with the idea of personal freedom. Furthermore, is it necessary to have the shackles of religious observance to be a good Jew or, for that matter, a good person? There are thousands of Jews who are good, moral and decent human beings, yet non-observant. They engage in acts of kindness both within the Jewish and non-Jewish communities. They lead active lives and many are role models in the worlds of science, art and commerce, yet they do not keep *Shabbat*, lay *Tefillin* etc. What is wrong with being a good but non-observant Jew?

The good life

We all wish to live a good life. Most of us think that this means having the best of what life has to offer: a good and supportive family, good parents, a good spouse, good children and grandchildren. A good income and home. A good environment and community, good friends, and –

Can One Be a Good Jew Without Being Religious?

most important – having a good time. A sum total of all good things equals a good life. A person starting out in life is faced with the puzzling question of how to create this good life.

And what a great puzzle it is. Taking a look around us we see that life is far from perfect and full of pitfalls. In today's modern fast-moving world, more and more children are born into broken homes, more couples are splitting up and more people are suffering from depression and lack of self esteem. More people are discovering that material wealth does not ensure the road to happiness. More people are taking pills, drugs and tranquillisers. You have to be very lucky indeed to hit the jackpot and have all the factors in place to create the good life. In the end most of us settle for mediocrity, acknowledging that you can't have everything in life, a somewhat sobering but pragmatic conclusion. What is, therefore, the secret of the good life?

G–d is Good

G–d, the Creator of man, who is also Creator and Master of the whole world, surely has the best qualifications that might be expected of any authority to know what is good for man and for the world in which he lives. G–d has not withheld this knowledge from us. G–d is good and it is the nature of good to be good. In His infinite kindness He has communicated to us that if a person conducts his life in a certain way he will have a healthy soul in a healthy body, and it will be good for him in this world and in the World to Come. It just makes plain common sense that in order to have a good life one should follow the directives of the Creator of man, even if there are aspects of those directives which superficially seem restrictive.

An analogy may be drawn from a car. Before one steps into a car it is highly advisable to consult the manual in order to achieve the best performance levels from the car. Anyone who ignored the instructions could damage the car and, in some cases, the driver as well.

In truth there are many things in daily life which a person accepts and follows without question, even if he be a highly gifted intellectual with a searching bent of mind. For example, a person will board a plane without having first researched aerodynamics to verify that it is safe to fly in and that it will bring him to his destination at the scheduled time.

To take an example from the area of physical health: there are drugs which are known to be useful or harmful to one's health and a person would not go about trying to verify the utility or harmfulness of such a drug through personal experimentation. Even if a person had a very strong inclination to research and experiment, he would surely choose those areas which have not previously been researched.

This generally accepted attitude is quite

understandable and logical. For, inasmuch as experts have amply researched these areas and have determined what is good and what is harmful for physical health, or have established the methods leading to further technological advancement, it would be a waste of time to repeat those experiments from the beginning. Furthermore, there is no assurance that some error may not be made leading to the wrong conclusions being drawn, possibly with disastrous effects.

What has been said above concerning physical health is also true in regard to spiritual health, and the means by which the soul can attain perfection and fulfilment. All the more so, since spiritual health is generally related to physical health, particularly insofar as a Jew is concerned.

It is quite certain that if a human being would live long enough, and would have the necessary capacities to make all sorts of experiments without distraction, interference or error, he would undoubtedly arrive at the very same conclusions which we already find in the Torah; namely, the need to observe *Shabbat*, *Kashrut* etc. The reason for this is that the Torah is the truth and the ultimate good for a person.

But G–d, in His infinite goodness, wished to spare us all the trouble, as well as the possibility of error, and has already given us the results beforehand for the benefit both of those who have the inclination and capacity to search as well as for those who do not. G–d has definitely left areas where a person can carry on his own experiments in other areas which do not interfere with the rules laid down by Him.

Stated simply, the directives of the Torah are not a set of rules that have been given to impede or restrict the freedom of man. Rather, they are the pathway to a good life.

Let us take a few examples.

A person who works seven days a week leaves no time to recharge his spiritual batteries. Even limited leisure time is often devoted to keeping the body fit at gyms, health clubs or golf courses while the soul goes sadly neglected. To most people the severe restrictions of *Shabbat* appear to be limiting factors. In truth, those restrictions create an atmosphere and ambience that allows – in some cases, gently forces – a person into a totally different set of circumstances that enhance personal and familial spiritual growth.

A fictional story is told of a bird during the days of creation. This particular bird was created without wings and when it looked around at other birds soaring in the heavens it implored the Creator to allow it to fly. That night, whilst the bird was asleep, G–d affixed wings to its body. When the bird awoke and saw two new appendages to its body it said to G–d, "G–d, I asked you to make me fly, not to make me heavier." G–d replied, "little bird, just flap them and you will see that you will fly." The restrictions often seem like extra baggage but once we utilise them, they allow us to fly and soar into new heights.

The Rabbis tell us that "there is no free man except he who engages in the study of Torah." This simply means that the Torah frees a person from personal restraints. Superficially this seems surprising, for the Torah places many restrictions on a person. The answer is that in every generation and age there is a form of bondage; an "Egypt". Some people are slaves to their jobs, others to the desires of their body. Some worship money, others power. Torah is the antidote that frees a person from his personal bondage. It manoeuvres a person into the enviable position of being able to maximise the goodness of this world, as well as the next.

G–d is not an ogre or ruthless dictator who insists on His subjects keeping a meaningless routine. G–d is benevolent and good and wishes to bestow good upon His creation. The greatest act of Divine benevolence was to give us a living Torah – a pathway through life which leads us to the greatest good a human may achieve both for his body and soul.

In short, if a person wants to have good relationships with his parents, spouse or children he should follow the directives of the Torah. If he wants to have a healthy body he should follow the laws of *Kashrut*. If he wants to create healthy children he should keep the laws of *Taharat Hamishpachah* (the laws of family purity). If he wants to have a healthy mind and heart he should lay

Tefillin and study Torah. To create a healthy atmosphere at home he should create a home where Torah is studied and *mitzvot* are kept. If he wants family dialogue he should have a Friday night table upon which words of Torah are discussed. If he wishes to be protected he should have a *mezuzah* on his door. If he wishes for Divine benevolence he must dispense charity to the needy. These are the pathways, not only to bliss in the World to Come, but also to a meaningful and fulfilling life in this world.

In describing how a Jew must accept the commandments, the Rabbis often use the expression "acceptance of the yoke of *mitzvot*", which may imply that the *mitzvot* are somewhat of a burden. However, the true meaning of this expression is to be understood in the sense that human nature makes it necessary to act on imperatives. For human nature and the *Yetzer Hara* (evil inclination) are such that an individual might easily succumb to temptation. Temptation is sweet at the beginning but bitter at the end and human nature may lead an individual to disregard the bitter consequences because of the initial gratification. We see, for example, that children, and very often adults also, may be warned that over-indulgence in certain foods would be harmful to them and may even make them so ill that for a period of time they may not be able to eat anything at all, yet they nevertheless reject all restraint to gratify their immediate appetite. In a like manner G–d has given us the "yoke" of Torah and *mitzvot*, telling us that whether one understands them or not, or whatever the temptation may be, one must carry out G–d's commandments unquestioningly.

The Divine bridge

There is a further point, and this is the most essential part of the concept of "yoke" of the Torah and *mitzvot*. It is that although the Torah and *mitzvot* have been given for the benefit of man, there is an infinitely greater quality with which G–d has endowed the Torah and *mitzvot*. This is the quality of uniting man with G–d – that is, the created with the Creator – with whom he would otherwise have nothing in common. For, by giving man a set of *mitzvot* to carry out in his daily life, G–d has made it possible for man thereby to attach himself to his Creator and transcend the limitations of time and space.

The Torah and *mitzvot* constitute the bridge which spans the abyss separating the Creator from the created, enabling the human being to rise and attach himself to G–dliness. This bridge has been designed by G–d, for only He can span that abyss. It is quite impossible for a limited being to create his own bridge to the Infinite, for whatever bridge he may build, however spiritual it may be, it will still be limited according to the parameters of the created mind. This explains why a person cannot create his own path to G–d independent of Torah and *mitzvot*. Torah is a revelation from Above, "And G–d came down on Mount Sinai". It is He who reached out to us and provided the path to Him.

Of course this relationship can only be attained if the person observes the Torah and *mitzvot*, not because of the reward contained therein, whether for the body or the soul, but purely because it is the will and command of G–d. It is for this reason that the text of the blessing which a Jew makes before fulfilling a *mitzvah* does not mention the utility of the *mitzvah*, rather the fact that G–d has sanctified us with His commandments and commanded us.

The very word "*mitzvah*" means both a commandment and a connection. The 613 commandments are 613 connections that the human being may form with G–d. The *mitzvot* span the entire spectrum of human experience and give man the opportunity to sync with the Divine in both his spiritual and mundane affairs.

In fact, the essence of Judaism is belief in a Creator who brings the entire creation into existence from nothing every single second. His purpose is to create a physical world in which a person will create a fitting abode for the Divine. This is achieved by connecting every aspect of the creation with the Creator. In short, *mitzvah* performance.

Even in man's most mundane activities he must connect with G–d. Before eating he must recite a blessing, realising who is the Creator of the food. Whilst honouring parents he must realise that this is the fifth commandment and equal to honouring G–d.

The rabbis teach, "The reward for a *mitzvah* is a *mitzvah*." Some commentaries explain this in the literal sense that the reward for a *mitzvah* is the opportunity to perform another *mitzvah*. However, in the light of the above, one may explain that the reward of a *mitzvah* is the very connection that the person has with his Creator whilst he is doing the *mitzvah*.

This connection is life itself. In a Jewish context life may be defined as something eternal, whereas death is something that is interrupted. The Rabbis teach that the righteous, even in death, are alive. The pleasures of this world are momentary. They may last for a minute, an hour, a week, or even a few years but, after a while, are gone. Life – true life – is eternal. When engaging in *mitzvah* performance, a person is connecting with G–d, and therefore with eternity itself, and so is truly alive. That connection lasts forever and stands above time. The righteous are alive even after death because their entire focus in this world is their connection with G–d which continues even after death.

This leads us to the true definition of happiness. Ultimate happiness may not be gauged by any amount of self-gratification, even of a spiritual nature. True happiness may be defined as the knowledge that one is doing the will of G–d at any given moment. Such happiness is constant and permanent. A person may serve G–d with joy even when going through difficult moments. That attachment is, in fact, the true goodness that a person may experience, for it is an experience of G–d Himself. In fact, the greatest good that G–d could possibly give us is Himself.

To explain further: The world is a creation by G–d and, as such, can have no common denominator with its creator. This world consists of a variety of creatures which are generally classified into four "kingdoms": minerals, vegetation, animals and mankind. Taking the highest individual of the highest group of the four, i.e. the most intelligent of all men, there can be nothing in common between him – a created and limited being – and G–d – the Infinite Creator.

However, G–d gave us the possibility of approach and communion with Him by showing us the way that a finite created being can reach beyond his inherent limitations and commune with the Infinite. Obviously, only the Creator Himself knows the ways and means that lead to Him, and only the Creator Himself knows the capacity of His creatures in using such ways and means. Herein lies one of the most essential aspects of the Torah and *mitzvot*. Although, to many, the Torah may be a means to gain reward and avoid punishment or just a guide to good living, being G–d given it has infinite aspects, and one of the most important is that it provides the means whereby we may reach a plane above and beyond our status as created beings. Clearly, this plane is far beyond the highest perfection which a man can obtain within his own created – and hence limited – sphere.

From this point of view it no longer appears strange that the Torah and *mitzvot* find expression in such simple, material aspects as in, for example, the Dietary laws. For our intellect is also created and therefore limited within the boundaries of creation beyond which it has no access. Consequently, it cannot know the ways and means that lead beyond those bounds. The Torah, on the other hand, is the bond that unites the created with the Creator, as it is written, "And you that cleave to G–d, your G–d, are all living this day." To the Creator all created things, the most corporeal as well as the most spiritual, are equally removed. The question, "what relationship can a material object have with G–d?", has no more validity than if it referred to the most spiritual thing in its relationship to G–d.

The beauty of Torah and *mitzvot* is that through simple everyday actions – well within the reach of normal individuals – every person can connect with the Divine and transform this world into an abode for G–d. The Torah is not in heaven, rather, "it is exceedingly near to you, in your mouth and in your heart to do it."

What about a compromise?

This is also the answer to those who seek a compromised Judaism – selecting which *mitzvot* they will or won't keep. Approaching Torah and *mitzvot* on a selective basis is a contradiction in terms. If a person reserves the right to decide what to observe and what not to observe then the whole Torah ceases to be for him a Divine instrument. Surely, it is far more honest ethically to be aware of the Torah's standards and to aim towards them, trying one's best, than to cut down Judaism's standards to suit convenience.

Now let us return to the original question – can a person be a good Jew without being observant? The answer is that even if a person lives what he personally considers to be a good and moral life and engages in acts of kindness etc., although he is partially fulfilled through the *mitzvot* he is doing (and living a good and moral life is truly desirable in the eyes of G–d), he is nonetheless denying himself the maximum and optimum goodness available and so missing out on a very precious opportunity.

The true meaning of good

One last point. In truth, without the Torah, which illuminates and gives directives to our rather complicated and rushed lives, we could possibly err as to what good means.

Self-evident moral precepts, if left to human judgement without the binding force of Divine direction and sanction, can out of self-love be distorted so as to turn vice into virtue. Interpreting the moral precepts of "Thou shalt not kill ... Thou shalt not steal" from the viewpoint of selfish gain, many a nation, as well as many an individual, have "legalised" their abhorrent ends, not to mention justifying the means to those ends.

If in a previous generation there were people who doubted the need of Divine authority for common morality and ethics in the belief that human reason is sufficient, our present generation has unfortunately, in a most devastating and tragic way, refuted this mistaken notion. For it is precisely the nation which excelled in the exact sciences, humanities and even in philosophy and ethics, that turned out to be the most depraved nation of the world, making an ideal of robbery and murder. Anyone who knows how insignificant was the minority of Germans who opposed the Hitler regime realises that the German cult was not something which was practised by a few individuals but it had embraced the vast majority of that nation, which considered itself the "super-race".

From this blatant historic example it is obvious that moral standards cannot be determined by individuals alone, for their human partiality will colour their values. Rather, humankind should rely on a more absolute standard of goodness and morality which is set out by G–d in the values of the Torah.

One of the basic messages of the Ten Commandments is contained in their opening words, "I am the L–rd your G–d" – the profound principle of monotheism which, in itself, was a tremendously revolutionary idea in those days of idolatry, dominated by the polytheistic culture of Egypt. This is detailed in the second commandment where all forms of idolatry are strictly prohibited. At the same time, the Ten Commandments conclude with such apparently simple and obvious injunctions as "Thou shalt not steal" etc.

The profundity of monotheism, with which the Ten Commandments begin, and the simplicity of the ethics and moral laws with which they conclude, point to two important lessons:

1. The true believer in G–d is not the one who holds abstract ideas, but the one whose knowledge of G–d leads him to the proper daily conduct even in ordinary and commonplace matters, in his dealings with his neighbours and respect for their property.
2. The ethical and moral laws, even those that are so obvious as "Thou shalt not murder" and "Thou shalt not steal", will have actual validity and be observed only if they are based on the first and second commandments; that is to say, based on Divine authority, the authority of the One and only G–d.

The Ten Commandments emphasise, and experience has fully and repeatedly borne out, that even the simplest precepts of morality and ethics must rest on the foundation of "I am G–d" and "Thou shalt have no other g–ds" and only then can their compliance be assured. Torah and *mitzvot* alone provide the true content of Jewish life and are at the same time the fountains of life for each and every Jew.

In summary
1. A life of Torah and *mitzvot* is the surest path to a good life. It is the very best thing for a human being and will bring him to the greatest fulfilment in this world.
2. The greatest good a person may experience is G–d Himself. This connection is achieved through Torah and *mitzvot*.

7

Are Science and Religion a Contradiction?

In the traditional view of the Bible, the world is a mere five and a half thousand years old and was created in six days. Surely modern science proves that the world is billions of years old and man evolved through a process of evolution, thus laying to rest the Biblical story of Genesis? Can one honestly follow antiquated religious beliefs when science proves otherwise?

The definition of science and religion

Science, broadly defined, means knowledge. Specifically we refer to science as knowledge ascertained by observation and experiment, critically tested, systemised and brought under general principles. Being even more specific one must distinguish between empirical or experimental science dealing with, and confined to describing and classifying, observable phenomena, and speculative science dealing with unknown phenomena, sometimes phenomena that cannot be duplicated in the laboratory. The term "scientific speculation" is actually a terminological incongruity since no speculation can be called knowledge in the strict sense of the word. At best, scientific speculation can only describe theories inferred from certain known facts and applied in the realm of the unknown.

Religion means a belief in something. In terms of the Jewish religion this is belief in the Divine nature of the Torah – *Torah min Hashamayim*; that the Torah received by Moshe and given to the Jewish people is Divine in source and is the word of G–d. Being so, Torah is Divine wisdom, and since G–d is true so is his Torah. Torah is often referred to as *Torat Emet* meaning the True Torah. Torah reveals the truth.

From these two definitions we see that science formulates and deals with theories and hypotheses while Torah deals with absolute truths. These are two different disciplines and "reconciliation" is entirely out of place. Torah is the realm of truth of the absolute. What Torah says is true not because it has been scientifically proven to be true, rather it is true because the truth was revealed by G–d. Science does not deal with absolutes, rather it deals with the realm of observable phenomena and produces principles based on its observations.

The science of yesterday & the science of tomorrow

In the 19th Century it was the prevailing view of scientists and modernists that human reason was infallible in "scientific" deductions and that sciences such as physics, chemistry, mathematics etc., were absolute truth, that is to say, not merely accepted truths but absolute. Speaking in Jewish terms this meant the establishment of a new idolatry, not of wood and stone, but the worship of the contemporary sciences and philosophies.

In fact, in the face of dogmatic and deterministic views of science prevailing at that time, a whole apologetic literature was created by well-meaning religious advocates and certain rabbis who saw no other way of preserving Torah heritage in their "enlightened" communities except through tenuous and spurious reinterpretations of certain passages in the Torah in order to accommodate them to the prevailing world outlook. No doubt they knew inwardly that they were suggesting interpretations in Torah which were at variance with *Torat Emet*, but at least they felt they had no alternative.

In the 20th Century, however, and especially in recent decades, science has finally come out of its medieval wrappings and the whole complexion of science has changed. The assumed immutability of the so-called scientific laws and the concept of absolutism in science in general have been abrogated and the contrary view is now held, known as the "Principle of Indeterminism". Nothing any more is certain in science but only relative or probable, and scientific findings are now presented with considerable reservation and with limited and temporary validity, likely to be replaced at any time by a more advanced theory.

Most scientists have accepted this principle of uncertainty – enunciated by Werner Heisenberg in 1927 – as being intrinsic to the whole universe. The 19th Century dogmatic, mechanistic and deterministic attitude to science is gone. The modern scientist no longer expects to find truth in science. The current and universally accepted view is that science must reconcile itself to the idea that, whatever progress it makes, it will always deal with probabilities, not with certainties or absolutes.

Let us give two examples of the metamorphosis of scientific discovery. There is a verse in Ecclesiastes 1:4, "The earth stands forever", that seems to suggest that the earth stands still and the sun revolves around the earth. This presentation was entirely acceptable in the early common era, especially when, in the second century, Ptolemy perfected Aristotle's construction of how the sun and the planets revolve around the earth in circular orbits with additional rotation around certain points on these orbits.

That view was adopted by all scientists and especially amongst religious clergy who viewed the earth as the centre of the universe. About 1,500 years later Nicholas Copernicus made a revolution in astronomy by describing the earth as going around the sun. Suddenly this new scientific discovery threw all religious belief into disarray. Even today in most schools children are taught that the earth revolves around the sun and that this is a fact proven by science. To suggest otherwise is considered unscientific.

However such education is prejudiced since Albert Einstein's Theory of Relativity eliminated the idea of absolute space and absolute movement. According to Einstein, science in principle cannot decide whether the earth stands still and the sun revolves around it, or *vice versa*. In *The Philosophy of Time* by Hans Reichenbach, a disciple of Einstein, he demonstrates that all the following concepts are clearly shown possible from a scientific point of view:

1. The earth stands still and the sun revolves around it,
2. The sun stands still and the earth revolves around it,
3. Both are revolving around a certain point. There is no way to prove which of the above is correct or preferable.

For practical purposes it is simpler to calculate astronomical events if we assume that the sun is standing still and the earth is moving around it. Copernicus' main motive was to make calculation easier but this is not good enough reason to ascribe "truth" to this concept. To dismiss the Biblical verse that suggests that the earth stands still is wholly unscientific.

The problem with the science *v* religion debate is as previously mentioned – that most people accepted scientific discovery as absolute, which precluded and excluded religious belief. Even today, some eighty years after the theory of relativity was published, although scientists accept the theory in their professional capacities, they ignore it in the context of philosophical debate, preferring to support old-fashioned ideas of absolutism. They continue to be governed by ideological preconceptions, blindly opposed to Torah, which have been absorbed into their consciousness since childhood, even when these preconceptions contradict professional knowledge.

Another good example of an ever-changing theory is that of light. The ancient Greeks developed a "corpuscular" theory of light, i.e. that light is a flux of tiny particles emanating from a source and moving linearly in all directions. The theory of geometrical optics was developed on the basis of this assumption. This theory successfully served mankind for centuries in designing and building lenses, prisms, flat and curved mirrors, vision aids, and later microscopes, telescopes, and other optical systems. Then it was discovered that light also follows a wavy motion and so it was reinterpreted as electromagnetic waves of a very short wavelength. Scientifically, the corpuscular theory developed into a wave theory. In the beginning of the 20th Century, Albert Einstein suggested that, in fact, light possesses a dual nature, i.e. the unification, in one entity, of two opposite concepts of a particle of matter and of a wavy motion. This new idea became the basis of the new fundamental theory of quantum mechanics.

It is most interesting to note that the Kabbalah uses light as a metaphor for the power of G–d. It speaks in terms of the *Or Ein Sof* – the Infinite light. One of the principles of faith is that G–d is omnipotent and may carry opposites. The fact that light possesses a dual nature and can carry an opposite makes it the perfect metaphor for Divine energy. In this third stage of the development of the light theory it becomes apparent that this unification of two concepts underlines the unity of G–d within creation. (See "The Lubavitcher Rebbe on Science and Technology" by Professor Herman Branover in *B'Or Ha'Torah*, Vol.9)

The age of the universe

A problem that bothers many is the seemingly irreconcilable contradiction of science claiming the world to be billions of years old and the Torah view that the world is 5,763 years old (at the date of this publication).

Furthermore, this contradiction has led some well-meaning religious scientists to reinterpret the passages of Genesis to the effect that the days of creation refer to periods or aeons, rather than ordinary days. They suggest that since the sun, moon and stars were only "hung in the sky" on the fourth day of creation, therefore the 24 hour day could not have come into effect until at least

Are Science and Religion a Contradiction?

the fourth day. Furthermore, they claim, if one were to ascribe vast periods of time to each of the days of creation, all the theories of evolution and the Big Bang could fit in quite nicely with the Torah.

However such interpretation tampers with the commandment of *Shabbat* – a *mitzvah* which is considered by our Sages to be equivalent to keeping the entire Torah. For, if one takes the words "one day" out of context and plain meaning, one *ipso facto* abrogates the whole idea of *Shabbat* as the seventh day stated in the same context. The whole idea of *Shabbat* observance is based on the clear and unequivocal statement in the Torah, "For in six days G–d made heaven and earth, and on the seventh day He ceased from work and rested" – days, not periods.

As previously mentioned, such attempts at reinterpreting the Torah are, of course, the outmoded legacy of the 19th Century. Nowadays there is surely no justification whatsoever to perpetuate this "inferiority complex". Certainly there is no basis for holding on to views which have come down in outdated elementary and high school textbooks on science.

It is very saddening to think that those who should be the champions of the Torah outlook and its advocates, especially among Jewish youth in general, and academic youth in particular, are timid or even ashamed to expostulate it.

The above is not meant to belittle science or the

scientific method, rather there must be a differentiation between ephemeral science and theories drawn from scientific speculation. This is in contrast to Torah, which is eternal and immutable. When the Torah is modified or altered by compromise, to whatever extent, it ceases to be the truth. And the truth remains the same for all people and for all times. If one accepts the eternity of the Torah, and this can only be on the basis of *Torah min Hashamayim*, then it would be absurd to say that, while it is true that Torah was given by G-d, times have changed, as if the Creator and Governor of the universe could not have foreseen that there would be a 21st Century when certain groups of people, such as scientists or "modernists", would be inclined to accept only a compromised Torah, not the Torah of truth.

Let us now inspect more closely the methods scientists have employed to discover the age of the universe. Science has two general methods of inference:

1. The method of interpolation (as distinguished from extrapolation), whereby, knowing the reaction under two extremes, we attempt to infer what the reaction might be at any point between the two.
2. The method of extrapolation, whereby inferences are made beyond a known range, on the basis of certain variables within the known range. For example, suppose we know the variables of a certain element within a temperature range of 0 to 100 and, on the

basis of this, we estimate what the reaction might be at 101, 200 or 2,000.

Of the two methods, the second is clearly the more uncertain. Moreover, the uncertainty increases with the distance away from the known range and with the decrease of this range. Thus, if the known range is between 0 and 100, our inference at 101 has a greater probability that at 1,001.

Let us note at once that all speculation regarding the origin and age of the world comes within the second and weaker method. The weakness becomes more apparent if we bear in mind that a generalisation inferred from a known consequent to an unknown antecedent is more speculative than an inference from an antecedent to consequent as can be demonstrated very simply.

Four divided by two equals two. Here the antecedent is represented by the divided and divisor, and the consequent by the quotient. Knowing the antecedent in this case gives us one possible result – the quotient – number two.

However, if we only know the end result, namely the number two, and we ask ourselves how can we arrive at the number two, the answer permits several possibilities, arrived at by different methods: $1 + 1 = 2$, $4 - 2 = 2$, $1 \times 2 = 2$, $4 \div 2 = 2$. Note that if other numbers come into play the number of possibilities giving us the same result is infinite (since $5 - 3 = 2$, $6 - 4 = 2$ etc., *ad infinitum*.)

Add to this another difficulty which is prevalent in all methods of deduction: Conclusions based on certain known data, when extended to unknown areas, can only have validity on the assumption of "everything else being equal", that is to say, on an identity of prevailing conditions and their action and counter-action upon each other. If we cannot be sure that the variations or changes would bear at least a close relationship to the existing variables in degree, if we cannot be sure that the changes would bear any resemblance in kind, if, furthermore, we cannot be sure that there were not other factors involved – such conclusions of inferences are absolutely valueless!

For further illustration, in a chemical reaction, whether fissional or fusional, the introduction of a new catalyst, however minute the quantity, into the process may change the whole tempo and form of the chemical process or start an entirely new process.

Now the whole structure of science is based on observances of reactions and processes in the behaviour of atoms in their present state as they now exist in nature. Scientists deal with conglomerations of billions of atoms as these are already bound together and as these relate to other existing conglomerations of atoms. Scientists know very little of the atoms in their pristine state – of how one single atom may react on another single atom in a state of separateness – much less of how parts of a single atom may react on other parts of the same or other atoms. One thing science considers certain is that the reaction of single atoms upon each other is totally different from the reaction of one conglomeration of atoms on another.

We may now summarise the weaknesses of so-called scientific theories regarding the origin and age of the universe:

1. These theories have been advanced on the basis of observable data during a relatively short period of time of only a number of decades; at any rate, not more than a couple of centuries.
2. On the basis of such a relatively small range of known (though, by no means, perfectly known) data, scientists venture to build theories by the weak method of extrapolation, and from the consequent to the antecedent, extending to, according to them, millions and billions of years!
3. In advancing such theories they blithely disregard factors universally admitted by all scientists, namely that in the initial period of the "birth" of the universe, conditions of temperature, atmospheric pressure, radioactivity, and a host of other catalystic factors, were totally different from those existing in the present state of the universe.
4. The consensus of scientific opinion is that there must have been many radioactive elements in the initial stage which now no longer exist, or exist only in

minimal quantities; some of them elements the catalystic potency of which is known even in minimal doses.

5. The formation of the world, if we are to accept these theories, began with a process of colligation (binding together) of single atoms, or the components of the atom, and their conglomeration and consolidation, involving totally unknown processes and variables.

In short, all of the weak "scientific" theories, those which deal with the origin of the cosmos and with its dating, are, by the scientists' own admission, the weakest of the weak.

It is small wonder (and this, incidentally, is one of the obvious refutations of these theories) that the various "scientific" theories concerning the age of the universe not only contradict each other but, in some cases, are quite incompatible and mutually exclusive since the maximum date of one theory is less than the minimum date of another.

If anyone accepts such a theory uncritically it can only lead him into fallacious and inconsequential reasoning. Consider, for example, the so-called evolutionary theory of the origin of the world, which is based on the assumption that the universe evolved out of existing atomic and sub-atomic particles which, by an evolutionary process, combined to form the physical universe and our planet on which organic life somehow developed, also by an evolutionary process, until *homo-sapiens* emerged. It is hard to understand why one should really accept the creation of atomic and sub-atomic particles in a state – which is admittedly unknowable, and inconceivable – yet be reluctant to accept the creation of planets, or organisms, or a human being, as we know these to exist.

The argument from the discovery of fossils is by no means conclusive evidence of the great antiquity of the earth, for the following reasons:

1. In the view of the unknown conditions which existed in "prehistoric" times, as already mentioned – conditions which could have caused reactions and changes of an entirely different nature and tempo from those known under the present day orderly processes of nature – one cannot exclude the possibility that dinosaurs existed over 5,000 years ago and became fossilised under terrific natural cataclysms in the course of a few years, rather than over millions of years, since we have no conceivable measurements or criteria of calculations under these known conditions.

2. Even assuming that the period of time which the Torah allows for the age of the world is definitely too short for fossilisation, one may readily accept the possibility that G–d created ready fossils, bones or skeletons (for reasons best known to Him), just as he could create ready living organisms, a complete man,

and such ready products as oil, coal or diamonds, without any evolutionary process.

As for the question, if the latter reason is true, why did G–d have to create fossils in the first place? The answer is simple: We cannot know the reason why G–d chose this manner of creation in preference to another, and, whatever theory of creation is accepted, the question will still remain unanswered. The question, "why create a fossil?", is no more valid than the question, "why create an atom?" Certainly, such a question cannot serve as a sound argument, much less as a logical basis, for the evolutionary theory.

What scientific basis is there for limiting the creative process to an evolutionary process only, starting with atomic and subatomic particles – a theory full of unexplained gaps and complications – while excluding the possibility of creation as given by the Biblical account? For, if the latter possibility be admitted, everything falls neatly into a pattern and all speculation regarding the origin and age of the world becomes unnecessary and irrelevant.

It is surely no argument to question this possibility by saying, why should the Creator create a finished universe, when it would have been sufficient for Him to create an adequate number of atoms or sub-atomic particles with the power of colligation and evolution to develop into the present cosmic order? The absurdity of this argument becomes even more obvious when it is made the basis of a flimsy theory, as if it were based on solid and irrefutable arguments overriding all other possibilities.

Evolution

First and foremost let it be stated that the theory of evolution has no bearing on the Torah account of creation. Even if the theory was substantiated and the mutation of species were proven in lab tests this would still not contradict the possibility of the world having been created as stated in the Torah rather than through the evolutionary process.

How much more so since the whole theory is highly speculative and, although, during the years of research and investigation since the theory was first advanced, it has been possible to observe certain species of animal and plant life of a short life span over thousands of generations, yet it has never been possible to establish a transmutation from one species to another, much less to turn a plant into an animal. Such a theory can have no place in the arsenal of empirical science.

The theory of evolution is a typical example of how a highly speculative and scientifically unsound theory captured the imagination of the masses and has allowed them to dismiss the Biblical account despite the fact that the theory has not been substantiated scientifically and is devoid of any real scientific basis. It is almost as if the sceptics were searching for a reason to disbelieve. Their misguided axiom was that the Bible is wrong and they needed some replacement theory. Evolution was perfect. It provided a G–dless theory of creation and fuelled the atheistic bent. In truth, that is highly unscientific; pure science must be based on ephemeral data.

Human nature has also affected the debate. Although the various theories attempting to explain the origin and age of the world are weak, they are advanced because it is a matter of human nature to seek an explanation for everything in the environment, and any theory, however far-fetched, is better than none, at least until a more feasible explanation can be devised.

One may well ask why, in the absence of a sounder theory, the Biblical account isn't accepted by the scientists? The answer is again to be found in human nature. It is a natural human ambition to be inventive and original. To accept the Biblical account deprives one of the opportunity to show analytic and inductive ingenuity. Hence, disregarding the Biblical account, the scientists must devise reasons to justify doing so and take refuge in classifying it with ancient and primitive mythology and the like, since it cannot be argued against on scientific grounds.

Converging not diverging

As time proceeds science will actually discover the

truths of the Torah. Rather than being seen as diverging, science and religion are converging. There is a story of a group of scientists who were climbing the mountain of creation. As they reached the summit they found a rabbi sitting and learning. He looked up from his book and said to the weary scientists, "I told you so!"

This fact has been predicted by the ancient Kabbalistic text, the Zohar. On the verse in Genesis 7:11, "In the six hundredth year of Noah's life ... all the fountains of the great deep were opened and the windows of the heaven were opened", the Zohar comments:

> In the six-hundredth year of the sixth millennium, the gates of wisdom from above will be opened as well as the fountains of wisdom from below, and the world will be prepared to be elevated in the seventh millennium.

The Zohar predicts that in the Hebrew year 5600, which corresponds to the year 1840 CE, there will be major developments both in the wisdom from above and the wisdom from below. The wisdom from above refers to esoteric wisdom in which major revelations were made in the dissemination of Chassidic philosophy starting in that year. It is well known that the founder of the Chassidic movement, the Baal Shem Tov, once, through mysterious Kabbalistic means, entered into the heavenly palace of the *Mashiach* and asked him, "When will the Master come?" *Mashiach* replied, "When the wellsprings of your teachings will be widely dispersed." The major developments in the teachings and dissemination of Chassidism that occurred after the year 1840 are a true fulfilment of that indication.

The wisdom from below refers to the major advances in science which also began around that time. The major industrial revolutions, which occurred in the mid 19th Century, paved the way for the major technological advances of recent years.

The connection between these two wisdoms is that they will converge. In the messianic era, it is prophesied (Isaiah 40:5) that, " … the glory of G–d will be revealed, and all flesh will see together that the mouth of the L–rd has spoken." As a preparation for the messianic revelation there will be an explosion in scientific discovery ultimately revealing the truth of the esoteric wisdom of the Torah.

Indeed, the discoveries in the natural sciences have thrown new light on the wonders of creation and the modern trend has consequently been towards the recognition of the unity pervading nature. In fact, with every advance in science, the underlying unity in the physical world has become more clearly discernible; so much so, that science is now searching for the ideal formula which would comprise all the phenomena of the physical world in one comprehensive equation.

Are Science and Religion a Contradiction?

With a little further insight it can be seen that the unity in nature is the reflection of true monotheism in its Jewish concept. For, as Jews conceive of monotheism, it is not merely the belief that there is only one G–d, but that G–d's unity transcends also the physical world, so that there is only one reality, namely G–d.

Indeed, the principle of unity is the essence of Judaism – since Abraham first proclaimed monotheism in a world of idolatry – which came to full fruition at the revelation at Mount Sinai. For true monotheism, as professed by us, is not only the truth that there is only one G–d and none with Him, but that there is "nothing besides" (*Ein Od*); that is, the denial of the existence of any reality but G–d's, the denial of pluralism and dualism, even of the separation between the material and the spiritual.

As noted previously, the more the physical sciences advance, the closer one approaches the principle of unity even in the world of matter. Formerly, it was the accepted opinion that the plurality and compositeness in the material world could be reduced to some hundred odd basic elements and entities, and physical forces and laws were regarded as being separate and independent, not to mention the dichotomy between matter and energy. However, in recent years, with the advancement in science, the basic elements themselves were reduced to several more elementary components of the atoms – electrons, protons, and neutrons – and even these were immediately qualified as not the ultimate "blocks" of matter, until the discovery was made that matter and energy are reducible and convertible into one another.

It is well known that the Baal Shem Tov taught, and Rabbi Shneur Zalman of Liadi explained and amplified, that every detail in human experience is an instruction in man's service to G–d. Thus, what has been said above about the advancement of science exemplifies also the progress of human advancement in the service of G–d. Man possesses two apparently contradictory elements, no less compatible than the incompatibility of matter and spirit, the counterpart of which in the physical world is matter and energy, namely the Divine soul and the animal soul, or, on a lower level, the *Yetzer Tov* (good inclination) and the *Yezter Hora* (the evil inclination). But this incompatibility is evident only in the infantile stage of progress in Divine service, comparable to the plurality of elements and forces which were presumed to exist in physical nature. Just as the appreciation of the underlying unity of nature grew with the advancement of science, so does perfection in the Divine service lead to the realisation of the essential unity in human nature, to the point where the *Yetzer Tov* and *Yetzer Hora* become one, through the transformation of the *Yetzer Hora* by and into the *Yetzer Tov*, for otherwise, of course, there can be no unity and harmony since all that is holy and positive and creative could never make peace and be subservient to the unholy, negative and destructive.

And in this attained unity the Jew proclaims, "Hear O Israel, G–d is our L–rd, G–d is one." This is also what our Sages meant when they said that the words, "And you shall love the L–rd your G–d with all your heart" (the words immediately following the *Shma*) mean: to love G–d with both your inclinations, with the *Yetzer Hora* as with the *Yetzer Tov*.

Conclusion

The intent of the above is not to cast aspersions on science or to discredit the scientific method. Science cannot operate except by accepting certain working theories or hypotheses, even if they cannot be verified, though some theories die hard even when they are scientifically refuted or discredited. No technical progress would be possible unless certain physical laws are accepted, even though there is no guarantee that the law will repeat itself. However, science can only deal with theories, not with certainties. All scientific conclusions or generalisations can only be probable in a greater or lesser degree according to the precautions taken in the use of the available evidence, and the degree of probability necessarily decreases with the distance from the empirical facts or with the increase of the unknown variables etc. Bearing this in mind one will realise that there can be no real conflict between any scientific theory and the Torah. On the contrary, a careful analysis of the findings of modern science and their philosophical meaning shows a convergence and harmony of science with Torah.

Many Jews today have become alienated from Torah and the Jewish way of life because of the tremendous, almost hypnotic, effect of a seemingly omnipotent science. Thousands justify their secularism by the "fact" that they are "more enlightened" than past generations. Many in the religious camp choose either to ignore (or ban) the discussion of the development of science and technology, or to adjust Torah to modern thought. In truth, neither approach is credible.

The correct approach is that there is no reason for the Torah observant Jew to be frightened by the science and technology explosion, or to take an apologetic position. He should always bear in mind the saying of the Zohar (Vol.1 p.161b), "G–d looked into the Torah and created the world." This means that the Torah is the blueprint of creation, and the finished product (the universe) cannot contradict the blueprint (Torah) by which it was designed.

By definition, Torah is Divine wisdom. The Torah is therefore the only ultimate source of true, complete and definitive knowledge about everything, including the objects and phenomena which science examines. Torah knowledge stems from a perspective "from Above", whereas scientific knowledge, obtained by the rational processing of empirical information, stems "from below".

Ultimately, these fountains will converge. We may look forward to the messianic era in which science, which in itself is neutral, will be elevated to serve for sacred purposes. Further scientific development and analysis will help us comprehend Torah concepts. Technology will bring the world to a situation where, as Maimonides describes the messianic era, "there will be neither famine nor war, neither envy nor competition, for good things will flow in abundance and all the delights will be as freely available as dust. The occupation of the entire world will be solely to know G–d".

8

What is Wrong with Intermarriage?

We live today in a multi-cultural and multi-religious society. We mix freely with, and respect, people of all faiths. Many Jews today grow up fully assimilated and comfortable in a secular society and environment. Why is it such a tragedy if a Jewish man finds a non-Jewish woman (or *vice versa*) with whom he feels totally compatible and decides to marry her? He claims that she is a genuinely lovely person with a fine character – often much nicer than any Jewish woman he has met. She is at home with his Jewish background and culture and both share the same values, hobbies and pursuits. A perfect match, yet not made in Heaven. Why not?

The decision to marry out is perhaps the most telling moment, when a person must consider what being Jewish actually means. Is being Jewish simply an accident of birth? Is there a difference between a Jew and a non-Jew? Can one retain full Jewish identity if married to a non-Jewish partner? What if one finds the perfect partner – loving, caring, considerate, good fun – but unfortunately non-Jewish? What means more in life – a happy marriage

What is Wrong with Intermarriage?

or one's religion? If one has found true love, does religion really matter?

Where do you come from?
No person just arrives on the scene. We are all the product of bygone generations; in the case of the Jews, descendants of Abraham, Isaac and Jacob. Jacob's family descended to servitude in Egypt and after 210 years was miraculously redeemed by G–d through Moshe, His faithful servant. The Children of Israel were subsequently constituted as a nation at the stand at Sinai – the Torah being their "wedding contract" with G–d. To date, Jewish history spans over 3,300 years. During this time Jews have had their golden eras and also have suffered severe persecutions, inquisitions, pogroms and, ultimately, the Holocaust. To be born a Jew today is not an accident of birth but the sum total of over 3,300 years of ancestral self-sacrifice, of heroes who at times gave their very lives for their beliefs. Somewhere along our ancestral line, you can be sure that a grandfather or mother had to accept poverty, hardship, derision, exile and humiliation, but stubbornly stuck to their faith. Greeks, Romans, Crusaders, Nazis and Communists all tried to obliterate Jewish practice and faith, but failed. The persecutors are all relics of the past but Judaism is alive and vibrant. The indomitable Jewish spirit survived and clung to its traditions despite all odds.

And now, the very latest link of that glorious tradition wishes to sever the chain in one fell swoop! Imagine if one were able to resurrect all one's ancestors. They would differ in language, dress and cuisine but all would share the same Jewish tradition. What would one say to a great-great-grandfather who sat in prison for keeping *Shabbat*? What would one say to a great-great-grandmother who would walk for miles to buy *kosher* provisions? How could one possibly introduce them to a non-Jewish fiancé?

A story was told by Mr. George Rohr, an American philanthropist, at a convention for the Lubavitcher Rebbe's emissaries in 1996. Mr Rohr related how he had the privilege to meet the Rebbe on one occasion just after *Rosh Hashanah*. Mr. Rohr thought it appropriate to present the Rebbe with a "spiritual" gift. A short time before, he had set up a beginners service at his shul in Manhattan, and on *Rosh Hashanah* 120 Jews attended this new service. Mr. Rohr decided to announce this to the Rebbe and was sure the Rebbe would receive much *nachas* from this good news. When his turn arrived, he confidently strode up to the Rebbe and said, "Thank G–d, this *Rosh Hashanah* we set up a beginners service in our shul and had 120 Jews with no Jewish background participate!"

Until that point the Rebbe had a broad smile on his face, but when Mr. Rohr told him the news the Rebbe's face dropped, and Mr. Rohr searched his words for anything he may have said that had upset the Rebbe.

"What?!" said the Rebbe.

Mr. Rohr repeated, "... 120 Jews with no Jewish background."

"No Jewish background?" asked the Rebbe. "Go and tell those Jews that they are all children of Abraham, Isaac and Jacob."

Now Mr. Rohr understood. The Rebbe objected to these Jews being described as having no Jewish background. Every Jew has a very illustrious background – they are all sons of Abraham, Isaac and Jacob!

This is all the more true after the Holocaust. Intermarriage is, in a sense, an act of treason to our people for, instead of bringing new Jews into the world by marrying a Jewish wife, one would be contributing to the decimation of our people and the "Final Solution" that Hitler and his followers began and nearly accomplished. The horrific rates of intermarriage today constitute a silent annihilation of our people.

The Chosen People

One may ask, however, is this not a guilt trip? After all why do *I* have to be liable to continue this chain, to pass on the traditions and to carry the baton just because my *mazal* was that I was born Jewish? Who placed this awesome responsibility on my shoulders? Furthermore, there are plenty of others who will carry on the traditions. What difference does it make if I sidetrack a little and shunt myself into a dead-end?

Every merit comes with responsibility and every responsibility comes with liability. At Sinai, G–d proclaimed us the Chosen People. Chosen for what?

Just before G–d gave the Ten Commandments he spoke to Moshe and said, (Exodus 19:5,6) "Now if you obey Me and keep My covenant, you shall be my special treasure among the nations, even though all the world is Mine. You will be a kingdom of priests and a holy nation to Me."

In these few words lies the task for which the Jews were chosen – to be a kingdom of priests. This means that every one of us must be holy in our private life, and in our association with the outside world every one of us, man or woman, must fulfil priestly functions. The priests' function is to "bring" G–d to the people and to elevate the people to be nearer to G–d. Every Jew and Jewess fulfils their personal and "priestly" duties by living a life according to the Torah.

The extent of one's duties is in direct proportion to one's station in life. It is all the greater in the case of an individual who occupies a position of prominence, which gives him an opportunity to exercise influence over others, especially over youth. Such people must fully appreciate the privilege and responsibility which

What is Wrong with Intermarriage?

Divine Providence vested in them to spread the light of Torah.

Jews are called *Bnai Yisrael*. The word *Yisrael* is an acronym for the phrase, *"Yesh Shishim Ribo Otiot LeTorah"* which means that there are 600,000 letters in the Torah. Every Jew is compared to a letter in a Torah scroll. Even if only one letter is missing the entire scroll is incomplete and invalid. Every Jew is an ambassador of his people in his echelon in society. That is his G–d-given responsibility and privilege. To shirk this responsibility is to deny oneself the ultimate privilege. To intermarry is an open violation of that responsibility.

Children

The Torah explicitly forbids intermarriage. The source is in Deuteronomy 7:3-4,

> You shall not intermarry with them; you shall not give your daughter to his son, and you shall not take his daughter for your son, for he will cause your child to turn away from after Me and they will worship the gods of others then the L–rd's wrath will burn against you, and He will destroy you quickly.

The direct implication is that children from such a union will be torn away from Judaism. Incidentally, this is also the Scriptural source for the law of matrilineal descent. Since the verse states "for he (ie a non-Jewish father) will cause your child to turn away ... ", this implies that a child born to a Jewish mother is Jewish whereas, if a Jewish man marries a non-Jewish woman, the child is not Jewish.

Thus, in the case of a Jewish man marrying a non-Jewish woman the child is not Jewish and an unbroken Jewish line has henceforth been broken. If a non-Jewish man marries a Jewish woman the children are Jewish. However the Torah explicitly forbids such a union for "he will turn your child away".

The truth is that a Jewish woman who has already married out and borne children should be encouraged to give them a full Jewish education. There are today thousands of practising Jews who only have a Jewish mother. However, to a couple contemplating intermarriage, the facts speak for themselves. Except in a small number of cases in which the mother is very determined and gives the child a very positive, strong Jewish education, in most cases the child grows up with a mixed and confused identity; in simple English, half-Jewish. Technically, there is no such thing – one is either 100% Jewish or not. However, in terms of identity, the child feels only half-Jewish. Even if the mother is a proud Jew, the father, whether atheist, agnostic, Protestant, Catholic, Muslim etc., does not share the same beliefs and values. Even if he is sympathetic, or even agrees to the child being brought up Jewish, there are bound to be differences. Does one celebrate *Chanukah* or Xmas, both or neither? Whichever one chooses is confusing or even contradictory. Many intermarried couples today celebrate both – but what sort of message does this give the child? Is the child Jewish, thus rejecting the notions of Christianity, or is the child a Christian with Jewish roots? It causes great confusion for the child and in many cases the child sees both faiths only on a superficial level, distanced by his parents from true belief.

The child is also given the test of mixed allegiances. All passages of life create a problem. Should the child be circumcised, christened, both or neither? Should the child have a *Bar Mitzvah* or be confirmed, marry in a synagogue or a church, be buried in a Jewish cemetery or be cremated?

And what chances are there that the child should want to marry a Jew? Even in the case of a determined Jewish mother who wishes to marry a non-Jewish partner and raise her child as a Jew, who says her child would want to marry a Jew and – most important – what sort of example has the mother set for the child?

Children learn from their parents. They cannot be taught ethics, they have to see them being practised. There is no sense in parents demanding that their child marry a Jew when one of the parents has married out!

There is another point: people are social beings. From time immemorial they have gathered in communities. One thing the international Jewish community prides itself in is the idea of *Kol Yisrael Chaverim* – all Israel are one fraternity, one brotherhood, one nation. If you are travelling to Bangkok and need a place for *Shabbat* you can be sure that if you turn up in shul you will get an invitation. Wherever a Jew goes he will have an international support group that extends hospitality and financial help, if needed. By having a non-Jewish child one has extricated the child from that community and bequeathed alienation to him. Everybody wants to belong – it is a basic human need. Intermarriage causes great confusion to children with regard to where they actually belong.

It's in the genes
Marriage in general, even between two people of similar background, entails a certain risk as to eventual adjustment and compatibility. Even if the two have been acquainted for some time there is no sure guarantee as to what the relationship will be like when the acquaintance is turned into a marriage, where the two will be thrown together under one roof for 24 hours a day, day after day and week after week. But when the backgrounds are entirely different, and where these differences date back for scores of

What is Wrong with Intermarriage?

generations – and are consequently of a deep and lasting quality – the chances of adjustment and compatibility are so negligible as to be almost non-existent. Especially where the differences are of a definitely antagonistic and hostile nature, as has been evidenced by the pogroms and persecutions of Jews in every land where Jews sojourned in the past 2,000 years. Moreover, modern science recognises the hereditary nature of character traits, particularly deeply rooted ones developed over generations.

Intermarriage usually results, sooner or later, in endless friction and unhappiness. That a casual, or even more serious, kind of relationship seemed in the past to indicate compatibility, is no proof that it would be so ever after in a marriage situation. On the contrary, it is inevitable that two people of such divergent backgrounds, one descending from generations of oppressed and victimised people the other from the world of the oppressors and predacious, should be affected by hereditary forces.

No change

Who says people don't change? Even if a couple are happy with each other, deeply in love, and have decided to marry despite their different religious backgrounds, who says that future events won't reverse their feelings? There are so many factors that can change a person's feelings.

King Solomon states, "I am sleeping but my heart is awake." A Jew may be sleeping spiritually but his inner Jewish heart is always awake and, at certain times, is aroused. Years into a marriage, where much of the relationship is routine, the soul and Jewish heart may be aroused to search for the deeper meaning to life. There may be a quest for spirituality and rediscovery of one's roots.

Consider the fact that these feelings will not be shared by your spouse. They will neither understand nor feel those same emotions and you will be alone. On the other hand, a Jewish partner means a shared history and a shared destiny.

But it works!
There is, of course, the argument that the percentage of intermarriages is considerable and many of them seem to last. However, the statistics show that the percentage of separations and divorces among intermarried couples is incomparably greater than among marriages within the faith. Secondly, many married people try to put on the appearance of a "happy" marriage, being ashamed to confess failure and to reveal the frictions and indignities suffered at home. In an intermarriage the sense of shame is even greater, knowing that many friends had warned against it, while the couple had maintained that their marriage would be different.

What is Wrong with Intermarriage?

It's simply not right

To be honest – in the plain sense of the word – one would not wish to drag another party into an alliance which is doomed from the start. If there is true love between the two parties, and not in a selfish way, one would certainly not wish to involve the other in such a misfortune, and would readily forgo the prospect of immediate and short-lived pleasure in order to spare the other the inevitable result. Otherwise the professed love is nothing but selfish and egotistic.

Should there be children from such a union, there is the added consideration of the tragedy of the children having to witness constant friction – and worse – between their parents, which is almost bound to follow in the natural course of events.

It is necessary to emphasise the point that one's personal convenience, desire or gratification is no justification for involving oneself with that which is wrong, especially to involve another person – least of all a loved one – into such a situation, even if the other person is agreeable, and sincerely so. No person has the right to harm another person.

A Jewish marriage

A Jewish marriage is called a *Binyan Adei Ad* – an everlasting edifice. In order that the edifice of marriage should indeed be strong and lasting, everything connected with the wedding, as well as the establishment of the couple's home, should be in full compliance with the instructions of the Torah. The Torah is called *Torat Chaim* – the Torah of life – it is the source of everlasting life in the Hereafter as well as the true guide to life on earth.

The analogy of marriage to an "everlasting edifice" is not merely a figure of speech but contains also an important idea and moral. In the case of any structure, the first and most important step is to ensure the quality and durability of the foundation. Without such a foundation, all the efforts put into the walls, roof, decorations and so on, would be of no avail. This is even more true of the structure of marriage; if its foundations are unstable, what tragedy could result! This is why a Jewish marriage must, first of all, be based on the rock- solid foundation of the Torah and *mitzvot*. Then the blessing of joy and happiness will follow the couple for the rest of their lives.

The Torah explicitly forbids intermarriage. Such a union has no foundation and will not be an everlasting edifice. In fact for a Jewish person to marry a non-Jew is one of the greatest calamities, and not only from the religious viewpoint. Nor is it entirely a personal matter affecting only the person involved, for it concerns the whole Jewish people, and there are few transgressions that affect the whole Jewish people as an intermarriage (G–d forbid) does. It is a transgression also against one's elementary honesty, for it is exceedingly unfair both to the other party and to the respective good friends, who wish to see their near and dear one lastingly happy.

Should I marry a Jewess just because she is Jewish?
Many young people feel themselves pressured by their parents to marry a Jewish spouse and, even though the choice is wider in the non-Jewish world, they feel obligated to marry within the fold out of a sense of duty. They often ask the question, what is the difference between the Jew and the non-Jew – both dress the same, both share common values, both eat the same food? If a man finds himself with a choice between two women, one Jewish and one non-Jewish, should he marry the Jewish woman just because she is Jewish?

The answer is a resounding "Yes!" Yes, because therein lies the potential for a truly Jewish marriage. Although at present there seems to be no difference between the Jew and non-Jew, as people grow older they change and mature. The vicissitudes, strains and challenges of life pull a person in all directions. If one is at least married to a Jew, there is common ground and potential to grow. That is certainly not the case in an intermarriage.

However, as strongly as the answer is yes, it carries an equally strong piece of advice. The institution of marriage – any marriage – needs much hard work. It is absolutely imperative that two young Jewish people who wish to marry should examine the huge repository of knowledge that the Torah has to offer to guide them in their future lives together. Couples must learn about the laws of *Taharat Hamishpachah* – the laws of Family Purity – that enhance the marriage. They must learn of the great importance of *Shalom Bayit* – peace in the home – and how to run a *kosher* home. They should learn about the importance of *chinuch* – education – even from an early age. No marriage can be taken for granted. As stated above, the foundation for a good marriage must be the Divine directives of the Torah, but a man and wife must understand that they have to work very hard to implement these directives in order to make the marriage successful.

Is conversion an option?

Conversion is serious business. Ask yourself a serious question: Is the conversion being carried out from a true desire to become Jewish, independent of any impending partnership, or is it a token conversion, done to please some parent? A serious conversion can take years and involves serious changes in lifestyle and conduct.

To undergo a "cosmetic" or "plastic" conversion is, obviously, no solution to a seriously minded person, and even more abhorrent to an honest person. A true conversion has to be such as to transform a non-Jew into a Jew, with a new Jewish *Neshamah* (soul), like a newborn child of Jewish parents. Such a conversion is one that is carried out in strict accordance with *Halachah*; anything less is only a sham and a mockery.

The *Halachah* is very clear in its insistence that the would-be convert honestly and wholeheartedly accepts all the *mitzvot*. Accepting all but one of the *mitzvot* automatically invalidates the conversion, and the non-Jew remains a non-Jew exactly as before. Of course, it is possible to mislead a rabbi or a Rabbinic Court by declaring one's readiness to accept all the *mitzvot*, but one cannot mislead the Creator who is the One who imbues the *Neshamah*.

There is the well known argument that it is unfair to demand more of a would-be convert, in terms of adherence to the *mitzvot*, than that which many born Jews observe in practice. This contention is inadmissible since it is a requirement and stipulation of Jewish Law to which the would-be convert must unequivocally commit himself.

A word of caution: within the Jewish community today one may convert in either an Orthodox or Progressive establishment. It should be clear from the start that an Orthodox conversion is accepted in all Jewish circles whereas the Orthodox do not accept a Progressive conversion. To convert in a Progressive establishment is hazardous in itself, for one's Jewish identity is not universally recognised.

It is analogous to a longer-but-shorter way. To get to

a particular destination one can take a long route but it may in fact be the shortest route. One may take a short route which might turn out to be a very long route. An Orthodox conversion is the longer-shorter way. It may be arduous and take a longer time but it is the shortest way to universal recognition. A Progressive conversion may be relatively easy but, in the final analysis, it is a very long route, for the end result is not recognised. It is a source of great shock to many children who find out that, since their parents underwent Progressive conversions, the Orthodox establishment does not consider them to be Jewish.

When a person marries he must be a little long-sighted. One cannot think just of oneself. One must take into consideration the status of one's offspring. Just as all parents wish to do the best for their child so, too, must all parents ensure that their offspring will not have any problems of Jewish status. Accordingly, anyone serious about conversion should consult a competent rabbinic authority. The reader is referred to the book *Who is a Jew* by Rabbi J.E. Schochet, which discusses this issue at length.

Advice to parents

Parents often seek rabbinical advice on how to stop an intermarriage.

In truth two pieces of advice are needed. One, before the crisis, and one after. When a child is born we wish the parents "*Mazal Tov*". In many cases, straight after the *Mazal Tov*, the parents put their newborn child's name down to attend the best schools in the area. One often hears from parents that they want to give their children the best education possible. By this they mean that they wish to expose their children to the highest levels of academia available in the secular world coupled with a weak pre-*Bar Mitzvah* education in the basics of Judaism. They expect their child to be worldly, educated, modern and open minded. They then pronounce that after such a broad education the child will be able to make his own choice about who he wishes to marry. When the child decides to intermarry the parents then run to the rabbi for a quick fix. Some parents resign themselves to the situation while others seek a token conversion.

In truth, such an education does not give the child free choice at all. If their choice is between a modern well-equipped science laboratory and an old stuffy synagogue classroom with a boring teacher – for sure they will choose the lab!

The story is told of a person who was asked if he knew what a *Tallit Katan* was. He replied affirmatively indicating on his own body the size of a pair of *Tzitzit* suitable for a seven year old – probably the type he once wore at Hebrew School. He was then asked what size suit he wore. When he appeared puzzled at the question it was explained to him that, since he now wears an adult size suit, why does he see himself in a child's size *Tzitzit*!

The point of this story is simple. The man's conception of Judaism is that of a child's because while in every other subject – Maths, English, History, etc. – he proceeded to higher education, in Judaism he stopped at *Bar Mitzvah*. No wonder he chooses to be assimilated since his choice appears to be between an adult modern world and an archaic irrelevant past.

If parents want to give their children a real choice, they have to give them a strong Jewish education and identity. It is only then that an informed choice can be made.

A father once came to a rabbi with his daughter and asked the rabbi to persuade her not to marry out. The rabbi asked the daughter why she didn't want to marry a Jew. She replied that her father never took her to synagogue, never ate *kosher*, never kept *Shabbat* or the festivals – in short, lived exactly like their non-Jewish neighbours, so why now the hypocrisy in demanding that she marry a Jew! The rabbi turned to the father and said that he agreed with her. The father was dumbstruck and then said that he had brought her to the rabbi to convince her not to marry out, and not to agree with her. The rabbi responded that, in order for her not to marry out, the father had to start living as a Jew. He suggested that the father should lay *Tefillin* daily and that his wife should start lighting the *Shabbat* candles. After a lot of persuasion the daughter eventually married a Jew.

To live as a Jew – that is the advice before the crisis, since prevention is the best cure. But what if one is already in a crisis?

Obviously parents should intensify their own efforts as well as enlisting the aid of friends to do everything to prevent the tragedy. When it comes to a Jewish heart one never knows when and how its innate Jewish feelings will be aroused. However, parents should consider the following:

All the members of a Jewish family constitute one organism and, when one part of it needs special treatment, it can be given in one of two ways; either directly, if possible, or indirectly, through strengthening other parts of the body, particularly those that govern the functions of the entire organism. The head of the family is called the *Baal Habayit* and the wife is called the *Akeret HaBayit*, corresponding to the heart of the family. Thus, strengthening the commitment to the Torah and *mitzvot* on the part of the parents has a beneficial effect upon all the members of the family. Of course, it may sometimes entail certain difficulties by having to make some changes, perhaps even radical ones, in regard to habits and lifestyle. On the other hand, considering the far-reaching benefits, and especially the fact that parents surely would not consider anything too difficult if it could be beneficial to their children, of what significance can any difficulty be, especially as in most cases these are often exaggerated? In any case, a Jew is always required and expected to live according to G-d's Will; how much more so when a special Divine blessing is needed.

At the same time there is the assurance that, however one's everyday life and conduct was in the past, a Jew can always start a new life through *Teshuvah* – which literally means returning to one's essence.

9

What is the Role of the Woman in Judaism?

In a Jewish household, the wife and mother is called in Hebrew *Akeret Habayit*. This means literally the "mainstay" of the home. It is she who largely determines the character and atmosphere of the entire home.

G–d demands that a Jewish home – every Jewish home – should have a Jewish character, not only on *Shabbat* and the holidays, but also on the ordinary weekdays and in "weekday" matters. It must be a Jewish home in every respect.

What makes a Jewish household different from a non-Jewish household is that it is conducted in all its details according to the directives of the Torah. Hence the home becomes an abode for G–d's Presence, a home for G–dliness, one of which G–d says, "Make Me a sanctuary, and I shall dwell among them." (Exodus 25:5).

It is a home where G–d's Presence is felt on every day of the week; and not only when engaged in prayer and learning Torah but also when engaged in very ordinary activities such as eating and drinking etc., in accordance with the directive, "Know Him in all your ways."

It is a home where mealtime is not a time for indulging merely in eating, but becomes a hallowed service to G–d, sanctified by the washing of the hands before the meal, reciting the blessings over the food, and Grace after the meal, with every item of food and beverage brought into the home being strictly *kosher*.

It is a home where the mutual relationship between husband and wife is sanctified by the meticulous observance of the laws and regulations of *Taharat Hamishpachah* (Laws of Family Purity, which include *Mikvah* attendance) and permeated with awareness of the active third "Partner" – G–d – in creating new life, in fulfilment of the Divine commandment, "Be fruitful and multiply." This also ensures that children are born in purity and holiness, with pure hearts and minds that will enable them to resist temptation and avoid the pitfalls of the environment when they grow up. Moreover, the strict observance of *Taharat Hamishpachah* is a basic factor in the preservation of peace and harmony (*Shalom Bayit*) in the home, which is vitally strengthened and fortified thereby – obviously, a basic factor in the preservation of the family as a unit.

It is a home where the parents know that their first obligation is to instill into their offspring, from their most tender age, the love, and fear, of G–d, permeating them with the joy of performing *mitzvot*. Despite their desire to provide their children with all the good

What is the Role of the Woman in Judaism?

things in life, Jewish parents must know that the greatest, indeed the only real and eternal legacy they can bequeath to their children, is to make the Torah, *mitzvot* and Jewish traditions their life-source and guide in daily life.

In all that has been said above, the Jewish wife and mother – the *Akeret Habayit* – has a primary role, second to none. It is largely – and in many respects exclusively – her great task and privilege to give her home its truly Jewish atmosphere.

She has been entrusted with, and is completely in charge of, the *kashrut* of the foods and beverages that come into her kitchen and appear on the dining table. She has been given the privilege of ushering in the holy *Shabbat* by lighting the candles on Friday, in ample time before sunset. Thus she actually and symbolically brightens up her home with peace and harmony and with the light of Torah and *mitzvot*. It is largely in her merits that G–d bestows the blessing of true happiness on her husband and children and the entire household.

In addition to such *mitzvot* as candle-lighting, separating *challoh* from the dough, and others which the Torah entrusted primarily to Jewish daughters, there are matters which, in the natural order of things, lie in the woman's domain. The reason for this being so in the natural order is that it stems from the supra-natural order of holiness, which is the source and origin of the good in the physical world. This refers to the observance of *Taharat Hamishpachah*, which by its very nature lies in the hands of the Jewish woman. The husband is required to encourage and facilitate this mutual observance; certainly not hinder it in any way, G–d forbid. But the main responsibility – and privilege – is the wife's.

This is the great task and mission which G–d gave to Jewish women – to observe and disseminate the observance of *Taharat Hamishpachah* and of the other vital institutions of Jewish family life. For besides being the fundamental *mitzvot* and the cornerstone of the sanctity of Jewish family life, as well as relating to the wellbeing of the children in body and soul, these pervade and extend through all Jewish generations to eternity.

It is to be remembered that the Creator has provided each and every Jewish woman with the capacity to carry them out in daily life in the fullest measure, for otherwise it would not be logical or fair of G–d to give obligations and duties which are impossible to fulfil.

It should be noted that the very Jewishness of a person is dependent on the mother. In Jewish law, if a person's mother is Jewish, then the person is Jewish. If only the father is Jewish, but the mother is a non-Jew, then the child is not Jewish. This very fact indicates the woman's primary role in preserving Jewish identity and values.

The above stated does not mean that the Jewish woman's place is solely in the home and that she should not follow a career. Rather it is the realisation that the primary role of the Jewish woman is that of a homemaker – the home and family unit being the nucleus of the Jewish community. Modern psychologists are affirming more and more what the Torah has always taught us: that a secure and loving home built on solid moral and ethical values is the basic building block of society. To pursue a career *at the expense* of shunning one's obligation and privilege in this area is misguided.

When a Jewish woman creates a Jewish home and educates her children in Torah and *mitzvot*, she is deserving of King Solomon's praise, "A woman of worth who can find ... a G–d fearing woman, she is to be praised."

Back to one's roots

Each and every Jewish woman is a descendant of the Matriarchs, Sarah, Rivkah, Rachel and Leah. It is incumbent on every Jewish woman to remember her roots.

In fact by reflecting upon the vital functions of roots in the world of plants one may deduce, by way of instructive analogy, a lesson for the contemporary Jewish woman.

The roots are the source of vitality of the plant from the moment of its birth when the seed takes root and thereafter, bringing it to fruition and constantly nourishing it throughout its life with the vital elements of water and minerals from the soil.

While the roots must also work for their own existence, growth, development and strength, their main function is to nourish the plant and ensure its full development, as well as its regenerative powers through the production of fruits and fruits of fruits. At the same time the roots provide a firm base and anchorage for the plant so that it will not be swept away by strong winds and other elements.

It is in the sense of these basic functions of physical roots that we can understand our spiritual roots. The "primary roots" of our Jewish people are our Patriarchs, Abraham Isaac and Jacob, as our Sages declare, "Only three are called *Avot* (Fathers)". On the maternal side our primary roots are our Mothers, Sarah, Rivkah, Rachel and Leah. Each of these founders and builders of the House of Israel contributed a distinctive quality which, blended together, produced the unique character of our Jewish people.

Most typical – and original (in the sense of parentage) – is the Patriarch Abraham, of whom it is written, "One was Abraham", for he was the only one in his generation who recognised the unity of G–d and, with complete self-sacrifice, proclaimed the Unity of G–d (pure monotheism) to a world steeped in polytheism and idolatry.

His progeny, the Jewish People, is still unique in carrying on his work – a small minority in a world which has many gods. It is from him that we inherited, and derive strength from, the quality of *Mesirat Nefesh* (self-sacrifice) as well as the supreme obligation to pass on our heritage to our children; for it was his greatest merit that, through his devotion and total dedication to G–d, "he bequeathed to his children and household after him to keep the way of G–d."

By referring to our Patriarchs as "roots" our Sages indicate a further essential aspect of roots that goes beyond the role of parents. To be sure, parents give birth to children and transmit to them some of their own physical, mental and spiritual qualities. However, children are not directly dependent on their parents for survival; they can move away from their parents and from their parental home, and will continue to thrive after their parents are gone. This is not so in the case of a plant and its roots. The roots are absolutely indispensable to the plant's existence and their vitalising influence must flow continuously to keep the plant alive and thriving. In the same way, our

Fathers and Mothers must always vitalise and animate our own lives.

Every Jew and Jewess should realise that he or she is an integral part of the great "root system" that began with our Patriarchs and Matriarchs and continued to thrive through the ages, nourishing and sustaining our people, whom G–d calls "a branch of My planting, the work of My hands, to take pride in them."

Yet, sad to say, there are some Jews who, for one reason or another, are not aware of their roots, and some whose roots have become so atrophied as to be in danger of becoming withered (G–d forbid). It is therefore up to the healthy plants and roots to work all the harder to revive and strengthen the others, and help them rediscover their identity and place within the root system of our unique people.

In this life-saving work, the role of the Jewish woman is of crucial importance since she is the *Akeret Habayit*, the foundation of the home, who largely determines the character and atmosphere of the household, and the future of the children in particular.

In the same vein, there can be no greater fulfilment for a Jewish girl than to prepare herself for her vital role of building the House of Israel as a worthy descendant of the Matriarchs. As indicated above, it is a dual process: actively pursuing one's own growth and development and at the same time working for the preservation and growth of our people, through spreading and strengthening *Yiddishkeit* in the Jewish community at large, particularly in areas where Jewish mothers and daughters can contribute most such as *Kashrut*, *Taharat Hamishpachah*, candle-lighting etc.

Finally, to pursue the roots analogy to one more significant point: one does not look for flashing colour and external beauty in roots, nor are the latter concerned with what some people might say about their external looks. Roots do their work humbly and modestly, indeed, for the most part, hidden from view altogether. Such is also the work of true Jewish mothers and daughters.

In a world where fashion and vogue hold sway, and where expediency often takes precedence over eternal values and principles, our worthy mothers and daughters are not concerned with what some neighbour or passer-by might say about the way they conduct themselves and their homes in accord with the laws of our sacred Torah. If these appear "old-fashioned" to the onlooker with his "modern" ideas of "new morality", we Jews take pride in our "old-fashioned" – yet always new and eternal – roots; we strive to become ever more root-like and ever more true to the primary roots of our Jewish people, whom G–d designated as a "Kingdom of priests and a holy nation."

True Jewish wealth
We would do well to remember the chassidic saying:

> Neither property nor money is the true Jewish wealth. The everlasting Jewish wealth is: being Jews who keep Torah and *mitzvot* and bringing into the world children and grandchildren who keep Torah and *mitzvot*.

10

Belief After the Holocaust

Sixty years on, people still ask the same questions – Where was G–d during the Holocaust? How can you believe in G–d after the Holocaust? If G–d is just and righteous how could He allow the Holocaust to happen? Why didn't G–d perform miracles during the Holocaust?

Who is asking the question?

The questions themselves can only be asked by a believer for if the answer is that there is no G–d (G–d forbid), then there are no questions. Without a G–d, the world has no destiny and no purpose. Human beings may decide to act as they wish for there is no accountability. Super races may be formed and only the fittest will survive. In a G–dless world the Holocaust is not a theological question, rather a statement of how low man can stoop. The question becomes rhetorical – not, "where was G–d during the Holocaust?" but rather, "where was man during the Holocaust?"

The very fact that even those who claim they are non-believers incessantly ask where was G–d, is in fact the greatest proof that they too, deep in their hearts, believe there is a G–d, only they are aching for an answer to the question. To be more benevolent one may say that, in fact, they want to believe in G–d but the Holocaust poses a question of such dramatic proportions that they feel they cannot believe.

For the true believer there should be no questions. He quotes the verse (Deuteronomy 32:4,5), "The Rock! – perfect is His work, for all His paths are justice; a G–d of faith without iniquity, righteous and fair is He." His faith is not challenged by the fact that he does not understand, for which mortal being can truly comprehend the ways of the A–mighty?

However, the very fact that he is human and mortal, and terribly disturbed and upset, does make him question. Some incomplete response must therefore be supplied so that the believer may continue to serve uninterruptedly and undisturbed.

Faith *versus* tragedy

The conflict between tragedy and faith is not new. Anybody knowledgeable in Jewish history will realise that our people have undergone the most terrible persecutions and genocide at the hands of many oppressors. The believing Jew of 1940 knew about the pogroms, crusades, destruction of the Temples, he read out aloud on the *Seder* night, "In each generation they rise over us to destroy us", and yet it did not shake his faith. Anti-Semitism was nothing new.

The same method by which the Jew of 1940 knew about the past and yet kept his faith could be employed after the Holocaust. The philosophical question of "Shall the Judge of the earth not do justice?" applies just as much to the seemingly meaningless suffering of an individual as to that of six million individuals. If it could be dealt with on an individual basis before the Holocaust, it could be dealt with in the same way afterwards. The difference is one of quantity, but the quality of the question remains the same.

In truth however, Hitler's Final Solution was something novel in that few people believed that in the 20th Century, when civilisation had reached its intellectual and ethical peak, such genocide was conceivable. Public consensus, supported by the media, reassured us that we could no longer return to the Middle Ages. However, the philosophers and poets of Berlin, with their fine manners and high society, turned into the world's greatest murderers. The Holocaust was not only perpetrated by monsters, but connived at by an entire nation numbering close to one hundred million people.

The world was silent. One may add, not only silent but on the whole passive, sometimes comfortable with what was taking place, and happy that it was not they, only others, who were carrying out the atrocities.

If anything the story of the Holocaust shows clearly that man may not rely upon his own intellect and his own feelings for righteousness and justice. Those with the highest diplomas and university degrees were often accomplices, if not direct perpetrators, of cold-blooded murder. Man must be accountable. The command, "Thou shalt not kill", must be premised on "I am the L–rd your G–d."

Did the great believers question?

The question, "Shall the Judge of all the earth not do justice?" (Genesis 18:25), can be authentic and carry weight only when it bursts forth from the pained heart of a deep believer. The first to ask this question was our forefather Abraham, himself a man of great faith and the father of all believers, who when told to offer his beloved son Isaac as a sacrifice, did not question. "And Abraham rose early in the morning," – he rose to do G–d's Will with alacrity.

The first to ask the question, "why do the righteous suffer and the wicked prosper?" was none less than Moshe. Moshe – the very one who led us out of Egypt, split the sea, stood on Sinai, and heard the commands, "I am the L–rd your G–d, Thou shalt not have any other gods before Me", – also questioned. ("other gods" may also be a reference to human intellect and comprehension when it is made the final arbiter of man's ethical issues.)

The *Talmud* (*Menachot* 29b) relates that Moshe was shown how the great Rabbi Akiva suffered a tortuous death at the hands of the Romans. When Moshe saw them comb Rabbi Akiva's flesh with iron rakes he exclaimed, "Is this Torah and is this the reward!?" The answer that came from Above was, "Silence, thus has arisen in the thought (of G–d)".

The problem with Moshe's question was not that he verbalised a thought and was subsequently silenced. It was the content of Moshe's question that was silenced. This is rather disturbing for the reply to his question was superficially no reply. Moshe requested a rationalisation and yet he received a command. But in no way do we find that the question weakens Moshe's faith. On the contrary, it is only faith that allowed the great to overcome their trials and tribulations.

Jeremiah, who asked, "Why are the wicked successful in their ways?", continually exhorted the people to restore their faith in G–d. Job suffers horribly and is taunted by his friends. He questions but never loses faith.

It is no great surprise that all the great who questioned remained faithful. The question itself is based on a fundamental desire for justice. The premise of faith is that there is justice and that ultimately justice is carried out. This idea of justice stems from a superhuman source that stands above man's limited grasp and intellect. Therefore, when justice is not seen to be done the question rocks not only the intellect but the very core of the questioner. However, after a brief moment of pain and protest, the questioner realises that he is trying to fathom the unfathomable, and comprehend the incomprehensible, to grasp that which is higher than intellect with intellect. He soon realises that such a reaction has no place and, while suffering, retires in the knowledge that although he cannot at this moment comprehend what is going on, ultimately the Supreme Judge will execute justice. Through the question, and expression of pain, his faith is restored and strengthened.

The Judge of billions

Cursory reflection on the fact that G–d judges all men at all times reveals that the Judge of whom we talk is superhuman. Non-comprehension of His ways does not serve to disqualify Him but rather stems from our inability to understand His infinite wisdom.

Look for example at what happens in courts of law today. How many innocent people are imprisoned due to the shortcomings of the judicial system and its judges. How may guilty people walk freely in the street. The judges and their clerks frequently complain of being overworked and legislation places restrictions on their working hours. In contrast, the Judge of all the earth, works 24 hours a day, dealing with the five billion people on the face of the planet. Can man have the brazenness to question or even attempt to understand?

A primitive man in an operating theatre
Ultimately the human being realises his perception is finite.

Imagine taking a primitive man and somehow transporting him into a modern operating theatre to witness open-heart surgery. First he sees men in masks walk into the room. They are all dressed in green and are wearing gloves. Next a man sleeping on a bed is rolled into the room and one of the men dressed in green puts a mask over his face. Another man removes the sheet and asks for a scalpel. The primitive man watches in horror as the surgeon makes the incision.

With his zero knowledge of modern medicine, the man comes to the terrible conclusion that what he is witnessing is murder in cold blood. Where he comes from that is not how men are killed. They die honourably in combat, not killed whilst asleep! It all seems wrong to him. His sense of justice is aroused and he protests.

Try and explain to that man that the operation he is about to witness is, in truth, a life-saving operation, one that will give a new lease of life to the patient. Impossible – the man has not got the faintest idea of hygiene, let alone modern operating techniques. However you explain it to him, he sees it as murder. It would take weeks, months, or even years for him to comprehend.

On one level we are all primitive men in G–d's

operating theatre. Our comprehension of the operation is limited and we often accuse the Master Surgeon without comprehending that all operations are made for the good of the patient.

G–d is the ultimate of good. He is good and His nature is to do good. Even within pain and suffering there is some good, although that may be obscured from the sufferer. Our faith leads us to believe that the Surgeon knows what He is doing.

Was the Holocaust a punishment?

There are those who wish to suggest that the Holocaust was a punishment for the sins of that generation.

The Lubavitcher Rebbe rejects this view. He stated (*Sefer HaSichot* 5751 Vol.1 p.233):

> The destruction of six million Jews in such a horrific manner that surpassed the cruelty of all previous generations, could not possibly be because of a punishment for sins. Even the Satan himself could not possibly find a sufficient number of sins that would warrant such genocide!

> There is absolutely no rationalistic explanation for the Holocaust except for the fact that it was a Divine decree ... why it happened is above human comprehension – but it is definitely not because of punishment for sin.

On the contrary: All those who were murdered in the Holocaust are called *"Kedoshim"* – holy ones – since they were murdered in sanctification of G–d's name. Since they were Jews, it is only G–d who will avenge their blood. As we say on *Shabbat* in the *Av Harachamim* prayer, "the holy communities who gave their lives for the sanctification of the Divine Name ... and avenge the spilled blood of His servants, as it is written in the Torah of Moshe ... for he will avenge the blood of his servants ... And in the Holy Writings it is said ... Let there be known among the nations, before our eyes, the retribution of the spilled blood of your servants." G–d describes those who were sanctified as His servants, and promises to avenge their blood.

So great is the spiritual level of the *Kedoshim* – even disregarding their standing in *mitzvah* performance – that the Rabbis say about them, "no creation can stand in their place." How much more so of those who died in the Holocaust, many of whom, as is well known, were among the finest of Europe's Torah scholars and observant Jews.

It is inconceivable that the Holocaust be regarded as an example of punishment for sin, in particular when addressing this generation, which as mentioned before is "a firebrand plucked from the fire" of the Holocaust.

In short, one can only apply the words of Isaiah, "My thoughts are not your thoughts and My ways are not your ways, says the L–rd." (Isaiah 55:8)

The soul dimension

Judaism believes in the existence of a soul. This soul descends from the heavenly realms to inhabit the body for seventy or eighty years after which it returns to its Maker. The soul exists before it enters the body and exists after it leaves the body. Rabbi Shneur Zalman of Liadi in *Tanya* describes the soul as a "part of G–d above", a spark of G–dliness which inhabits the body in order to create an abode for the A–mighty in the world. Chassidic philosophy explains at great length the purpose of the descent of the soul and the purpose of creation.

Leaving aside any deep philosophy, even the simplest of beings understands that the body is corporeal and physical whereas the soul is ethereal and spiritual. He further understands that the sword, fire and water can have an effect on the body but no effect on the soul. Sticks and stones can hurt physical bones but they can't touch the soul. It is then obvious that the gas chambers and crematoria affected only the bodies of those martyrs but not their souls.

Furthermore, it is logical to regard the soul as the main component of the compound body and soul. Just as all will agree that the head is more important than the foot, so too are thoughts and feelings more important than flesh.

Based on these two premises, which are logical and can be easily understood, it is clear that the Holocaust only achieved the severance of body and soul but did not destroy the soul. On the contrary, the soul lives on long after the body has been destroyed.

Imagine if someone looked into a room and saw somebody crying. Would it be logical to conclude that the person in the room had spent all his life crying? Conversely, if someone looked into a room and saw somebody laughing, would it be correct to assume that this person spends all his life laughing? Such conclusions would be ridiculous. We all know that a person's life constantly varies, containing moments of laughter and tears.

The same is true of those in the Holocaust. The precise number of years they lived in this world must be viewed in the context of the continuum of the soul. Although they physically lived so many years – some longer than others and, in the case of children and babies, some only a very short time – in terms of the time scale of the soul, which lives for thousands of years, it is but a brief moment! True, when we view the Holocaust we see an intense moment of destruction, but should we therefore conclude that this state is that of the soul!

We do not have any first hand accounts of the

situation of the souls of the Holocaust in the World to Come, however the Torah does tell us that the position of those who died sanctifying G–d's name is great indeed. This we may deduce from the following episode:

It is mentioned in the book *Maggid Meisharim (Parshat Tetzaveh)* that Rabbi Yosef Karo, the author of the Code of Jewish Law, was due to merit giving up his life for the sanctification of G–d's Name but for some reason this was commuted and he did not merit to die thus. He lived on to become the leading Halachic authority of his generation and wrote the great Code of Jewish Law which we still follow today. And yet this amazing achievement is considered secondary to martyrdom in sanctification of G–d's Name. From this we see that martyrdom – and all those who perished in the Holocaust were martyrs, for they died because they were Jews – has merits of the highest order.

There is no question for the believing Jew that although the moment of *Kiddush Hashem* (sanctification of G–d's Name) was horrific in terms of both physical pain and suffering this did not affect the soul and, on the contrary, was but a brief moment in the life of the soul, through which it attained eternal elevation. It is frequently explained and emphasised in the Torah that life on this earth is only a preparation for the future and everlasting life in the World to Come. The Mishnah (*Avot* 4:21) states, "This world is like a vestibule to the future world; prepare yourself in the vestibule so that you can enter the banquet hall." If, during the time one is in the vestibule there has been a period of suffering whereby there will be an infinite gain in the "banquet hall", this will surely be worthwhile. It is impossible to describe the joys of the life of the soul in the World to Come for, even in this world while the soul is connected to the body, its life is on an infinitely higher plane; how much more so when the soul is no longer distracted by the body. The suffering in the "vestibule", which is no more than a corridor to the "banquet hall", is after all a temporary one, and the gain is eternal.

Furthermore, one of the fundamentals of our faith is that of the resurrection of the dead. There is absolutely no doubt that all of the *Kedoshim* of the Holocaust will rise at the resurrection. The many beautiful and bountiful years following the resurrection will certainly suffice to give them their full reward in this world for all they achieved and deserve.

Submission or prayer

If the Holocaust was a Divine decree why do we find the great Jewish leaders urging us to storm the gates of Heaven with prayer in order to avert any evil decree? Surely we should just submit ourselves to the wisdom of G–d and not object?

We find the Previous Lubavitcher Rebbe, who himself lived through the Holocaust, proclaiming that all must plead and cry before the A–mighty King to annul the evil decree of destruction. But of what use was the crying if this was the Divine will?

Furthermore, the *Mishnah* in *Avot* (4:17) teaches, "One hour of repentance and good deeds in this world is better than all the life of the World to Come; and one hour of bliss in the World to Come is better than all the life of this world." This means that if we could add the sum total of worldly pleasures it would not equal one hour in the World to Come. The spiritual bliss and rewards of the World to Come are incomprehensible and far surpass any worldly pleasure. And yet, since G–d created this world as the purpose of creation, in the words of *Tanya*, "to create an abode for G–d in this world", it follows that one hour of fulfilling our purpose in this world – involved in repentance and good deeds – is better than all the spiritual rewards of the World to Come.

If this is the case what justifies taking so many Jews away from this world, removing their opportunity of living a life of Torah and *mitzvot*? Which spiritual reward of the soul equals an hour of repentance and good deeds in this world?

Moreover, there is the law of *Pikuach Nefesh* (saving a life). This law states that everything must be done in order to save a life even for one extra moment. The holiest day of *Yom Kippur* may be desecrated in order to save a life. The law goes further to state that even the

High Priest when performing the service in the Holy of Holies must leave in order to save a human life. Not only is this permitted, it is mandatory!

Since human life is so precious, both from a halachic and from a philosophical viewpoint, why did G–d act thus? Why the Holocaust which wiped out six million so mercilessly?

We mentioned before that even the greatest believers questioned. We could possibly restate their questions in the following way:

They believed firmly in an Infinite and Omnipotent G–d, and they understood that everything G–d does is for good, yet they felt that since G–d is not limited, and the Master Physician can treat the patient in a number of ways, why did the operation take place by such a drastic method? Could G–d not have found another way to treat the patient? Wasn't there a different way to avoid all the pain? True, we may need the operation – for a reason G–d understands best – but why did He choose such operating techniques?

The storming of the Gates of Heaven with prayer was in order to avert the means by which the result of the operation was to be achieved. The plea was: please achieve your desired result using a more palatable method. Why such a bitter medicine?

And yet, as mentioned above, after the initial burst of pain, they concluded and pronounced, "The L–rd is righteous in all His ways."

Memorials or actions

We must never forget what happened. Remembering what Amalek did to us is a positive commandment. Our generation must always be reminded and fully aware of the events and consequences of the Holocaust. Particularly the great acts of *Kiddush Hashem*, not just of those who rose to fight but also of those who persevered in keeping the Torah in impossible circumstances.

But in addition to remembering, there is an equally, if not more, important response to the Holocaust. When Pharaoh in Egypt sought to destroy us, the Torah tells us, "But as much as they would afflict them, so they would increase and so they would spread out." The true response to the Final Solution is to build a true Jewish life and home. Hitler sought to annihilate us; we must respond by building a more committed and numerous Jewish world. In fact, too much dwelling on any tragic event, and particularly the devastating events of the Holocaust, can drain one's energy and induce pessimism. These may negatively affect the rebuilding of Judaism and Jewry, which requires elements of *Bitachon* (trust) and *Simchah* (joy).

A fascinating historical note

Three of the most tragic periods of the Jewish people were: after the destruction of the first Temple, after the destruction of the second Temple and in the Middle

Ages following the Crusades. How fascinating that in each of these three periods we witness a phenomenal growth in the development of the Oral Tradition. After the destruction of the first Temple lived the Men of the Great Assembly who added many rabbinic injunctions and institutions. After the second Temple came the writing of the *Mishnah* and *Talmud,* and in the Middle Ages the period of the *Rishonim* who added detailed commentaries on the earlier texts. That same pattern has been repeated in the post-Holocaust era in which there has been explosive growth in Torah learning and publication of Judaica.

We must not give our enemies the final solution. We must increase our study of Torah and performance of *mitzvot*, for ultimately the deed is the main thing.

11

How Does One Cope With Bereavement?

It is natural to ask the question "why?" in a time of anguish. One general answer, which is really self-evident though often hard to accept in a state of emotional distress, is that it is surely illogical to limit the Creator in His designs and actions to conform to the understanding of a created human being.

To cite a simple illustration: no one can expect an infant to understand the ideas and actions of a learned professor, although the latter was once an infant himself and the infant may have the potential even to surpass the professor in due course. How much more so, and incomparably, when it comes to the infinite intelligence of the Creator *vis-à-vis* the finite and limited intelligence of a created human being.

The difference between a created human being and his Creator is absolute. Our Sages declare that a human being must accept everything that happens, both occurrences that are obviously good and those that are incomprehensible, with the same positive attitude that "all that G–d does is for the good", even though it is beyond human understanding.

This is not such a great revelation but, as the Torah

says, it is difficult for a person to accept consolation in a time of grief.

Nevertheless, G–d has made it possible for human beings to grasp some aspects and insights into life and after-life. One of these revealed truths is that the *Neshamah* (soul) is a part of G–dliness and is immortal. When the time comes for it to return to Heaven it leaves the body and continues its eternal life in the spiritual World of Truth.

It is also a matter of common sense that whatever the direct cause of the separation of the soul from the body (whether a fatal accident, or illness, etc.,) it could affect only some of the vital organs of the physical body but not, in any way, the spiritual soul.

A further point, which is also understandable, is that during the soul's lifetime on earth in partnership with the body, the soul is necessarily "handicapped", in certain respects, by the requirements of the body (such as eating and drinking) Even a *Tzaddik* (righteous person) whose entire life is consecrated to G–d cannot escape the restraints of life in a material and physical environment. Consequently, when the time comes for the soul to return "home", it is essentially a release for it as it makes its ascent to a higher world, no longer restrained by a physical body and physical environment. Henceforth, the soul is free to enjoy the spiritual bliss of being near to G–d in the fullest measure. That is surely a comforting thought.

It may be asked, if it is a release for the soul, why has the Torah prescribed periods of mourning? But there is really no contradiction. The Torah recognises the natural feelings of grief that are felt by the loss of a near and dear one, whose passing leaves a void in the family. The physical presence and contact of the beloved one will be sorely missed. So the Torah has prescribed set periods of mourning to give vent to these feelings and to make it easier to regain the proper equilibrium and adjustment.

However to allow oneself to be carried away by these feelings beyond the limits set by the Torah – in addition to it being a disservice to oneself and to others, as well as to the *Neshamah* – would mean that one is more concerned with one's own feelings than with the feelings of the dear *Neshamah* that has risen to new spiritual heights of eternal happiness. Thus, paradoxically, the overextended feelings of grief which are due to the great love for the departed one actually cause pain to the loved one, since the *Neshamah* continues to take an interest in the relatives left behind, sees what is going on (even better than before) and rejoices with them in their joys, etc.

Inasmuch as the soul is eternal and is now in a state where it is not constrained by the body's limitations, it is fully aware of what is happening in the family. When it sees that it is a cause of grief over and beyond the bounds of mourning set by the Torah it is obviously distressed by it, and this in no way contributes to the soul's peace and blissfulness.

Even during the soul's sojourn in this life the real bond between people and members of a family is not a physical one but a spiritual one. What makes the real person is not his flesh and bones but his character and spiritual qualities. This bond remains and all those who loved the person dearly should try all the more to bring gratification and continuous spiritual elevation to the *Neshamah* through greater adherence to the Torah in general, and particularly in the realm directly related to the soul's passing. To observe what is prescribed for the period of *Shiva* but not extend it, similarly, in regard to the period of *Shloshim* (thirty days) but not beyond, and then to serve G–d through the fulfilment of His *mitzvot* as service should be – with joy and gladness of heart.

One thing the departed soul can no longer do is the actual fulfilment of the *mitzvot*, which can be carried out only jointly by the soul and body together in this material world. But this, too, can partly be overcome when those left behind do a little more *mitzvot* and good deeds in honour, and for the benefit, of the dear *Neshamah*.

Shiva is, of course, a period of sorrow and mourning for the soul of a near and dear one which has returned to the World of Truth. A Jewish soul is described in the Torah as "the lamp of G–d" since its purpose on this earth is to spread the light of G–dliness. Its departure from this earth is a cause for mourning as prescribed by the Torah. Yet, together with this, one must not forget that the soul is eternal. Nor must it be forgotten that even such a painful event comes from G–d so there can be no doubt that there is a good purpose in it.

But the essential purpose of *Shiva* is that "the living should reflect in his heart" (Ecclesiastes Ch.7:2). This means that those left behind should search their hearts and re-appraise themselves. They should attempt to improve themselves in areas of daily life which are real and eternal – i.e. Torah and *mitzvot*. Indeed, since the soul that ascended to Heaven has left a gap of discontinued good deeds here on earth, the immediate relatives and friends should make compensation for it through additional and extra efforts on their part.

12

What is the Jewish Belief About 'The End of Days'?

The term "End of Days" is taken from Numbers 24:4. This has always been taken as a reference to the messianic era and therefore we shall explore – albeit briefly – the Jewish belief in the coming of *Mashiach*.

What does the word *Mashiach* mean?
Mashiach is the Hebrew word for Messiah. The word Messiah in English means a saviour or a "hoped-for deliverer". The word *Mashiach* in Hebrew actually means "anointed". In Biblical Hebrew the title *Mashiach* was bestowed on somebody who had attained a position of nobility and greatness. For example, the High Priest is referred to as the *Kohen Hamashiach*.

In Talmudic literature the title *Mashiach*, or *Melech Hamashiach*, (the King Messiah) is reserved for the Jewish leader who will redeem Israel in the End of Days.

What is the belief in *Mashiach*?
One of the principles of Jewish faith enumerated by Maimonides is that one day there will arise a dynamic Jewish leader, a direct descendant of the Davidic

dynasty, who will rebuild the Temple in Jerusalem and gather Jews from all over the world and bring them back to the Land of Israel.

All the nations of the world will recognise *Mashiach* to be a world leader and will accept his dominion. In the messianic era there will be world peace, no more wars nor famine and, in general, a high standard of living.

All mankind will worship one G–d and live a more spiritual and moral way of life. The Jewish nation will be preoccupied with learning Torah and fathoming its secrets.

The coming of *Mashiach* will complete G–d's purpose in creation: for man to make an abode for G–d in the lower worlds; to reveal the inherent spirituality in the material world.

Is this not a utopian dream?
No! Judaism fervently believes that, with the correct leadership, humankind can and will change. The leadership quality of *Mashiach* means that through his dynamic personality and example, coupled with manifest humility, he will inspire all people to strive for good. He will transform a seemingly utopian dream into a reality. He will be recognised as a man of G–d with greater leadership qualities than even Moshe.

In today's society many people are repulsed by the breakdown of ethical and moral standards. Life is cheap, crime is rampant, drug and alcohol abuse are on the increase, children have lost respect for their elders. At the same time technology has advanced in quantum leaps. There is no doubt that today, if channelled correctly, man has all the resources necessary to create a good standard of living for all mankind. He lacks only the social and political will. *Mashiach* will inspire all men to fulfil that aim.

Why the belief in a human Messiah?

Some people believe that the world will "evolve" by itself into a messianic era without a human figurehead. Judaism rejects this belief. Human history has been dominated by empire builders greedy for power.

Others believe in Armageddon – that the world will self-destruct, either by nuclear war or by terrorism. Again Judaism rejects this view.

Our prophets speak of the advent of a human leader, the magnitude of whom the world has not yet experienced. His unique example and leadership will inspire mankind to change direction.

Where is *Mashiach* mentioned in the Scriptures?

The Scriptures are replete with messianic quotes. In Deuteronomy 30:1 Moshe prophesies that, after the Jews have been scattered to the four corners of the earth, there will come a time when they will repent and return to Israel where they will fulfil all the commandments of the Torah. The gentile prophet Bilam prophesies that this return will be lead by *Mashiach* (see Numbers 24:17-20). Jacob refers to *Mashiach* by the name Shilo (Genesis 49:10).

The prophets Isaiah, Jeremiah, Ezekiel, Amos, Joel and Hosea all refer to the messianic era. For full references the reader is referred to the book *Mashiach* by Rabbi Dr.I.Schochet. It is interesting to note that on the wall of the United Nations building in New York is inscribed the quote from Isaiah (Ch.11:6), "And the wolf shall lie with the lamb". Furthermore, it is clear from the prophets, when studied in their original Hebrew, that *Mashiach* is a Jewish concept and will entail return to Torah law, firmly ruling out any "other" messianic belief.

What sort of leader will *Mashiach* be?

Mashiach will be a man who possesses extraordinary qualities. He will be proficient in both the written and oral Torah traditions. He will incessantly campaign for Torah observance among Jews and observance of the Seven Universal Noahide Laws by non-Jews. He will be scrupulously observant and encourage the highest standards from others. He will defend religious principles and repair breaches in their observance. Above all, *Mashiach* will be heralded as a true Jewish King, a person who leads the way in the service of G–d, totally humble yet enormously inspiring.

What is the Jewish Belief About 'The End of Days'?

When will *Mashiach* come?

Jews anticipate the arrival of *Mashiach* everyday. Our prayers are full of requests to G-d to usher in the messianic era. Even at the gates of the gas chambers many Jews sang, "*Ani Maamin*" – I believe in the coming of *Mashiach*!

However, the *Talmud* states that there is a predestined time when *Mashiach* will come. If we are meritorious he may come even before that predestined time. This "end of time" remains a mystery, yet the *Talmud* states that it will be before the Hebrew year 6000. (The Hebrew year at the date of this publication is 5763.)

This does not rule out the possibility of *Mashiach* coming today and now if we merit it. It should be noted that many Torah authorities are of the opinion that we are in the "epoch of the *Mashiach*" and the Lubavitcher Rebbe stated on numerous occasions that the messianic redemption is imminent.

Could *Mashiach* come at any time in any generation?

Yes. In every generation there is a person who potentially could be the *Mashiach*. When G-d decides the time has arrived, He will bestow upon that individual the necessary powers for him to precipitate that redemption.

Any potential *Mashiach* must be a direct descendant of King David as well as erudite in Torah learning. It should be noted that many people living today can trace their lineage back to King David. The Chief Rabbi of Prague in the 16th Century, Rabbi Yehuda Loew (the *Maharal*), had a family tree that traced him back to the Davidic dynasty. Consequently, any direct descendant of the *Maharal* is of Davidic descent.

Maimonides, a great Jewish philosopher and codifier of the 12th Century, rules that if we recognise a human being who possesses the superlative qualities ascribed to *Mashiach* we may presume that he is the potential *Mashiach*. If this individual actually succeeds in rebuilding the Temple and gathering in the exiles then he *is* the *Mashiach*.

What exactly will happen when *Mashiach* comes?

Maimonides states in his *Mishnah Torah* – a compendium of the entire halachic tradition – that *Mashiach* will first rebuild the Temple and then gather in the exiles. Jerusalem and the Temple will be the focus of Divine worship and "From Zion shall go forth Torah, and the word of the L–rd from Jerusalem."

The *Sanhedrin* – a supreme Jewish law court of 71 sages – will be established and will decide on all matters of law. At this time all Jews will return to full Torah observance and practice. It should be noted that in this present age of great assimilation and emancipation an unprecedented return of Jews to true Torah values has taken place. This *"Baal Teshuvah"* phenomenon is on the

What is the Jewish Belief About 'The End of Days'?

increase and paves the way for a full return in the messianic era.

Will miracles happen?

The *Talmud* discusses this question and again arrives at the conclusion that, if we are meritorious, the messianic redemption will be accompanied by miracles. However, the realisation of the messianic dream, even if it takes place naturally, will be the greatest miracle.

According to some traditions G–d Himself will rebuild the third Temple. According to others it will be rebuilt by *Mashiach*, while others suggest a combination of the two opinions. Some suggest that there will be two distinct periods in the messianic era: the first, a non-miraculous period, leading on to a second miraculous period.

Maimonides writes, "Neither the order of the occurrence of these events nor their precise detail is among the fundamental principles of the faith ... one should wait and believe in the general conception of the matter."

What will become of the world as we know it?

Initially, there will be no change in the world order other than its readiness to accept messianic rule. All the nations of the world will strive to create a new world order in which there will be no more wars or conflicts. Jealousy, hatred, greed and political strife (of the negative kind) will disappear and all human beings will strive only for good, kindness and peace.

In the messianic era there will be great advances in technology allowing a high standard of living. Food will be plentiful and cheap.

However the focus of human aspiration will be the pursuit of the "knowledge of G–d." People will become less materialistic and more spiritual.

What are the birthpangs of *Mashiach*'s arrival?

The *Talmud* describes the period immediately prior to the advent of *Mashiach* as one of great travail and turmoil. There will be a world recession and governments will be controlled by despots. It is in this troubled setting that *Mashiach* will arrive.

There is a tradition that a great war will take place, called the war of Gog and Magog, and there is much speculation as to the precise timing of this war in relation to *Mashiach*'s arrival.

There is a tradition that Elijah the prophet will come to the world and announce the imminent arrival of *Mashiach*. However, according to other opinions, *Mashiach* may arrive unannounced. Elijah would then arrive to assist in the peace process. Some suggest that if the *Mashiach* arrives in his predestined time then Elijah will announce his arrival, but if *Mashiach* comes suddenly then Elijah will appear after *Mashiach* has come.

What is the Jewish Belief About 'The End of Days'?

As mentioned before, it is unclear as to exactly how these events will unfold. However, this uncertainty does not affect the general matter of *Mashiach*'s arrival.

When will the resurrection of the dead take place?

One of the principles of Jewish faith is belief in the resurrection of the dead. According to the *Zohar* – an early Kabbalistic text – the resurrection will take place forty years after the arrival of *Mashiach*. However, certain righteous individuals will arise with the coming of *Mashiach*. All the dead will be resurrected in the Land of Israel.

There is a small bone in the body called the *Luz* bone (some identify this bone as the coccyx) from which the body will be rebuilt at the time of resurrection. Our daily prayers are replete with requests for the resurrection and there are many customs connected with it. (See the book *To Live and Live Again* – SIE Publications)

What can be done to bring *Mashiach*?

In general, mankind must strive to perform more acts of goodness and kindness. The Jew is mandated to learn and be aware of the messianic redemption, and strengthen his faith in *Mashiach*'s ultimate and imminent arrival.

Charity is a catalyst for redemption and every day in our prayers we sincerely plead many times for the rebuilding of Jerusalem, the in-gathering of the exiles and the return to Torah observance under the leadership of *Mashiach*. The Lubavitcher Rebbe mounted a worldwide *Mashiach* campaign to heighten the awareness of *Mashiach*'s imminent arrival. The Rebbe constantly urged every Jew to prepare himself, his family and his community for the arrival of *Mashiach*. This can best be achieved by "living with *Mashiach*"; that is, by learning about *Mashiach* and yearning for his coming.

Summary

In conclusion, the Jew always was and remains the eternal optimist. Even in his darkest hour he hopes and prays for a brighter future – a world of peace and spirituality.

13

Doing or Understanding – Which Comes First?

This book attempts to address the questions that explore the core of Judaism. Yet another question is even more fundamental: should one place one's understanding before one's doing? Should a Jew ever make his understanding of the commandments or of G–d's ways conditional on their observance?

When we received the Torah and *mitzvot* at Sinai, the Torah states clearly that we accepted them on the basis of *Naaseh* – "we will do" – first, and then, *V'Nishma*, – "we will hear and understand". In other words, on the basis of unconditional obedience and readiness to fulfil G–d's *mitzvot*, regardless of our understanding them rationally. While we must learn and try to understand as much as possible, prior knowledge and understanding must never be a condition to living up to the guidelines which G–d has given us in regard to our conduct and our actual way of life.

First it is necessary to start observing the *mitzvot* and eventually we will almost certainly come to a better appreciation of their significance and truth. To approach this matter from the opposite direction; that is, to understand first and only then to do, is wrong on two scores. First, the loss involved in not performing *mitzvot* cannot be retrieved. Secondly, the very observance of the *mitzvot*, which creates an immediate bond with G–d, develops additional powers, the sooner to understand and appreciate them. Take, for instance, a person who is ill and for whom medicine has been prescribed by a specialist. Would it not be foolish to say that he should not take them until he knew how the medicine could restore him to good health? In the meantime, he would remain weak and ill and probably get even worse. It is senseless because the knowledge of how the medicine does its work is not necessary in order to benefit from it. Moreover, while taking it he will get a clearer head and better understanding to learn how the prescription helps him.

To expand on this theme, the world is a well co-ordinated system created by G–d in which there is nothing superfluous or lacking. There is one reservation, however: for reasons best known to the Creator He has given man free will, whereby man can co-operate with this system, building and contributing to it, or do the reverse and cause destruction even of things already in existence. From this premise it follows that a man's term of life on this earth is just long enough for him to fulfil his purpose; neither a day too short nor a day too long. Hence, if a person should permit a single day, or week, let alone months, to pass by without his fulfilling his purpose, it is an irretrievable loss for him and for the universal system at large.

The physical world as a whole, as can be seen clearly from man's physical body in particular, is not something independent and separate from the spiritual world and soul. In other words, we have not here two separate spheres of influence as the pagans used to think, rather we are now conscious of a unifying force which controls the universal system which we call monotheism. For this reason it is possible to understand many things about the soul from parallels with the physical body.

The physical body requires a daily intake of certain elements in certain quantities obtained through breathing and consuming food. No amount of thinking, speaking and studying about these elements can substitute for the actual intake of air and food. All this knowledge will not add one iota of health to the body unless it is given its required physical sustenance; on the contrary, the denial of the actual intake of the required elements will weaken the mental forces of thought and concentration. Thus it is obvious that the proper approach to ensure the health of the body is not by way of study first and practice afterwards but the reverse, to eat and drink and breathe which, in turn, will strengthen the mental powers.

Similarly, the soul and the elements which it requires daily for its sustenance are known best to its Creator. A healthy soul is first and foremost attained by the performance of *mitzvot*, and understanding of them may come later.

The conclusion from all the above is clear enough. For a Jew, every day that passes without living according to the Torah involves an irretrievable loss for him and for all our people, inasmuch as we all form a single unity and are mutually responsible for one another. It also has an effect on the universal order and any theories attempting to justify it cannot alter this in the least.

Believers, sons of believers

The Torah declares that Jews are "Believers, the sons of believers", meaning that in addition to one's own belief in G–d, one has the cumulative heritage of the faith of countless generations, beginning with our Father Abraham, the first believer, that the source of blessing is G–d, the Creator and Master of the universe. If a human being who introduces a certain system must give guidelines as to how the system works, how much more so is it to be expected that G–d would provide guidelines as to how a human being, and especially a Jew, must live. These guidelines

Doing or Understanding – Which Comes First?

were revealed at Sinai with the giving of the Torah and *mitzvot*, which were transmitted from generation to generation, not only in content but also in their exact terms. Thus the Torah provides the guidelines as to how Jews must conduct their lives, especially their family lives.

Since the Torah and *mitzvot* and the Jewish way of life comes from G–d and His infinite wisdom they are not subject to man's approval and selection. Human reason is necessarily limited and imperfect. Its deficiencies are obvious since with time and study it improves and gains knowledge and personal opinions may change.

In our long history we have had the greatest human minds possible who nevertheless realised their limitations when it came to the knowledge of G–d and His laws and precepts. We have had great thinkers and philosophers who not only fully accepted the Torah and *mitzvot* but have been our guiding lights to this day, while dissident groups and individuals either disappeared completely or, worse still, continued as painful thorns in the flesh of our people and humanity at large. Anyone who is familiar with our history requires no illustrations or proofs of this.

Accepting our sacred tradition unconditionally and without questions does not mean that there is no room for any intellectual understanding. Within our limitations there is a great deal which we can understand and with which we can further enrich ourselves provided the approach is right. For G–d in His infinite grace has given us insight into various aspects of His commandments, an insight which grows deeper as we practise them in our daily life and make them our daily experience. In this way the Jew attains true peace of mind and a harmonious and happy life, not only spiritually but also physically, and fully realises how happy he is to be son or daughter of this great and holy nation, the Jewish people.

Coping with doubt

For a human being to question G–d's reasons for His *mitzvot* is actually contradictory to common sense. If one accepts them as Divine commandments it would be presumptuous, indeed ridiculous, to equate human intellect with G–d's, which would mean limiting G–d's intellect to that of a human being. By way of a simple illustration, one would not expect an infant to understand the importance of nutrition as set forth by a professor who has dedicated his life to this subject, even though the difference between the infant and the professor is only relative in terms of age and education. There can be no such comparison between a created human being and the Creator, where the difference is absolute.

It should therefore be a matter of common sense to understand what the Torah explains clearly, that whatever doubts and difficulties a Jew may have in matters of Torah and *mitzvot* are only tests of his faith in G–d, and that a person is equipped with the capacity to overcome such tests and distractions. It would be illogical to assume that G–d would impose obligations which are beyond the human capacity to fulfil. Indeed, if one has more difficult tests, it only proves that he has greater capacities to overcome them.

Having feelings and thoughts which are not in accord with the Torah should not be surprising inasmuch as Rabbi Shneur Zalman of Liadi explains right at the beginning of the *Tanya* that every Jew also has an "animal soul" connected with the material body which is often the source of confusion and distraction, even to the point of blundering from the right path and robbing him of peace of mind. On the other hand, what makes it easier to deal with the situation is the fact that the Jew also posseses a Divine soul which is truly a part of G–dliness Above, and which is the essential and true aspect of the Jew. Hence it is not only possible to overcome these material distractions but, as our Sages declare, "One who is determined to purify himself receives aid from on High."

Above all, it is necessary to cultivate sincere and wholehearted confidence in G–d – as it is written, "Thou shalt be wholehearted with G–d thy G–d" – and thus eliminate all sorts of worries, anxieties and confusions. It develops a sense of security in that there is a L–rd and Master Who takes care not only of the world as a whole but also of each individual with loving care.

Of course if a person has questions and even doubts he must not feel any shame in asking for clarification, and certainly one should not keep any doubts within oneself but one should seek answers. However, there is the one condition that, whatever the questions and doubts may be, this must not affect one's simple faith in G–d and in His Torah and *mitzvot*, even if the answers have temporarily eluded one. This condition goes back to the day when the Torah was received at Sinai on the principle of *Naaseh* before *Nishma*, the guiding principle for all posterity. However, after *Naaseh* follows *V'nishma* for G–d, the Essence of Goodness, desires us to follow the path of Truth on the basis of faith, but then to follow it up with knowledge and understanding, for then the totality of the person is involved in serving G–d to the fullest capacity.

No hypocrisy

There can be no question of hypocrisy when a Jew learns Torah and conducts his life in accordance with the Torah and *mitzvot* even if some of his other actions or feelings do not always harmonise with his Torah study and observance. The incongruity lies not in

Doing or Understanding – Which Comes First?

acting according to the Torah and *mitzvot* but rather in acting contrary to the Torah and *mitzvot*.

This is clearly demonstrated by the statement of Maimonides that if a Jew is compelled by an external force to do a *mitzvah* he is not regarded as having done the *mitzvah* under coercion but as having fulfilled the *mitzvah* voluntarily. This is explained as follows. Inasmuch as every action has its roots in nature and natural disposition, the nature of a Jew is that he always desires to act in accordance with the Torah and *mitzvot*. However, sometimes there may be some circumstance which overshadows this desire or immobilises it, the Rambam calls this the *Yetzer Hara* (evil inclination), which always tries to find ways to prevent a Jew from behaving according to his real nature. Consequently, the physical force, or the threat thereof, used in order to compel the Jew to perform the *mitzvah*, is not a force that induces him to change his real attitude, rather it removes the circumstance preventing him from exercising his true will. Once the external constraint is removed the true innate will is free to reassert itself.

How to start

The Torah tells us that the conquest of the promised Holy Land was to take place by stages. The same applies, in a deeper sense, to the personal conquest of the self. In other words, when it comes to personal advancement in matters of *Yiddishkeit* the best method is sometimes in the way of a gradual conquest, step by step, and stage by stage, rather than by means of a drastic change. Of course there are certain situations and matters where a drastic change may be necessary but, by and large, steady progress is usually more effective than progress by fits and starts.

Epilogue

The Ten Mitzvah Campaigns

In the light of all we have said it is clear that "the deed is the main thing". Doing must come before understanding. To this aim we have included here a brief digest of the Lubavitcher Rebbe's ten point *mitzvah* campaign. The campaign focuses on ten specific *mitzvot* through the fulfilment of which the individual and the family will come to a greater appreciation of their Jewish heritage.

Love your fellow Jew
Rabbi Akiva (one of the great sages of the *Talmud*) explained that love of a fellow Jew is "one of the leading principles of the Torah". A campaign for *Ahavat Yisrael* means that we make an effort that our thought, speech and actions be permeated with a real concern and sensitivity for the wellbeing of our fellow Jews. The Baal Shem Tov taught that one should have *Ahavat Yisrael* even for a Jew one has never seen in one's life. The rationale behind this is explained in Ch.32 of *Tanya* (See the book *To Love a Fellow Jew* – SIE Publications).

Jewish Education

The campaign for Torah education seeks to involve any and every Jewish child in an educational programme that will teach him or her what it means to live as a Jew. Education is not only for children. Adults are encouraged to enroll in study groups and seminars commensurate with their background and knowledge.

Torah Study

Torah is the medium of communication through which G–d enables man to know and serve Him. The campaign for Torah study encourages every individual to set fixed times for Torah study every day so that our spiritual growth and development can be systematic and directed. Rabbi Shneur Zalman of Liadi explained that Torah study should be fixed not only in time but also in soul. It should be the vortex around which the entire spectrum of our day-to-day experience revolves.

Tefillin

The Torah describes *Tefillin* as a sign, a public statement of Jewish involvement. By donning *Tefillin* every day an individual gives expression to his basic feeling of Jewish identity and its importance to him. The *Tefillin* are placed on the arm, facing the heart, and on the head. This signifies the binding of one's emotional and intellectual powers to the service of G–d. The straps, stretching from the arm to the hand and from the head to the legs, signify the transmission of intellectual and emotional energy to the hands and feet, symbolising deed and action.

Our sages explain that the verse, "And all the nations of the world shall see that the name of G–d is called upon you, and they shall fear you", applies to *Tefillin*. *Tefillin* are a medium to bring safety and security to Jews in the present era and hasten the coming of the ultimate security which will be experienced when *Mashiach* comes.

The Rebbe instituted this campaign on the eve of the Six Day War and specifically requested that soldiers in the Israeli Defence Forces should lay *Tefillin* and that this would protect them in battle.

Mezuzah

"And you shall write them on the doorposts of your house and on your gates." (Deuteronomy 6:9, 11:20)

A *kosher Mezuzah* is a small parchment scroll, handwritten by an expert scribe, which contains two Biblical passages, one of them the *Shema Yisrael*. On the reverse side of the parchment are written the three Hebrew letters, *Shin* (ש), *Dalet* (ד), *Yud* (י). This is an acronym for the Hebrew words, שומר דלתות ישראל, meaning, "Guardian of the doors of Israel". A *Mezuzah* is affixed on the right side of every door of the home (except the bathroom) and it protects the inhabitants while in and out of the house.

A *Mezuzah* designates a house (or room) as Jewish, it reminds us of our connection to G–d and our heritage. By placing it on the doorpost we declare that this is a house or room where the word of G–d and his Torah influences our behaviour, thus rendering it a holy dwelling.

Both *Tefillin* and *Mezuzot* need to be certified as *kosher* by an authorised scribe. They also require regular checking. In many instances, when the Rebbe received a request for a blessing (particularly in health matters) he suggested that *Tefillin* and *Mezuzot* be checked.

Charity

We should give to others out of a sense of responsibility realising that what we have is also a gift from G–d, granted to us with a purpose, so that we will help others. Our prosperity is a trust which we must steward and generously share with those in need. The *Tzedakah* campaign calls for an increase in giving as well as the conspicuous display of a *Tzedakah* box to serve as a reminder to give often every weekday. And our sages told us, "*Tzedakah* is great, because it brings the redemption near."

A home filled with Jewish books

An environment teaches. What you have in your home helps determine what type of home you will have. By having sacred Jewish books conspicuously displayed at home you, your family and visitors will be prompted to use them. Moreover, their very presence reminds us of their contents and the importance of Jewish values. Of course the more books the better. However, the minimum of a *Chumash* (the Five Books of Moses), a Book of Psalms and a *Siddur* (prayer book) is suggested.

Candle-lighting

Shabbat is a day of light; a day with a different pattern and value orientation from our ordinary weekdays. Every *Shabbat* is a foretaste of the era of *Mashiach*. The lighting of the *Shabbat* candles 18 minutes before sunset ushers in and inspires this state of awareness. The responsibility for lighting the candles and inducing this change of perspective is the woman's. It is she who welcomes the *Shabbat* Queen into the home. Young girls from the age of three are also encouraged to light their own candle so that they too can have a share in creating this environment.

Kosher food

Eating *Kosher* food enables us to identify with our Jewishness on a very basic and fundamental level. As long as our Jewish involvement is limited to prayer, study, or even specific ritual acts, it is spiritual, above our normal day to day reality. When you eat differently because you are Jewish your commitment is not only metaphysical, but part and parcel of your very being.

The observance of *Kashrut* consists of eating only *Kosher* foods both at home and away from home. It also entails not eating dairy and meat foods together and maintaining separate dishes, cutlery, and utensils for meat and dairy.

Family Purity
Taharat Hamishpachah – the attitudes and practices the Torah prescribes for married life – help to develop genuine communication and love between husband and wife and bring to the world healthy and loving children. Couples from all walks of life have adopted this *mitzvah* as a means to enhance and enrich their married life. A rabbi should be consulted as to the details of these laws.

Glossary

Ahavat Hashem – Love of G–d.

Ahavat HaTorah – Love of Torah.

Ahavat Yisrael – Love of a fellow Jew.

Baal Shem Tov – Lit. "owner of a good name" – a reference to Rabbi Israel ben Eliezer, the founder of the chassidic movement.

Baal Teshuvah – Repentant, one who returns to Jewish practice.

Brachah – Blessing.

Chabad – An acrostic formed from the initial letters of the words *Chochmah*, (wisdom), *Bina*, (comprehension), *Da'at* (knowledge). Generally used to describe the intellectual approach of the Lubavitch movement.

Chassid – (plural: chassidim): Follower of the Rebbe, adherent of the chassidic life style.

Chassidut – chassidic philosophy.

Galut – exile.

Halachah – Torah law.

Haggadah – Passover book for the *Seder*.

Hashem – G–d.

Kabbalah – "Inner" esoteric depths of Torah; mysticism.

Judaism Key FAQs

Kashrut – Observance of the kosher laws; dietary propriety of foods by Torah law.

Kiddush – Blessing of sanctification for *Shabbat*

Lubavitch – a town in White Russia, centre of the Chabad-Lubavitch movement for over a century.

Mashiach – Messiah.

Mezuzah – Parchment-scroll, inscribed with two paragraphs of Torah; affixed to doorpost.

Midrash – Rabbinic commentary and explanation.

Mikvah – Immersion pool built to rigid specifications of Torah-law; used primarily by married women as part of "Family Purity" laws.

Mishnah – the earliest compilation of the Oral tradition.

Mitzvah (plur: mitzvot) – Precept or command of Torah.

Moshe – Moses.

Nachas – Joy, usually from children.

Neshamah – Soul.

Pesach – Passover.

Rebbe – leader and head of the chassidim.

Rishonim – the early commentaries on the Talmud.

Seder – Lit. "order" – a reference to the celebration of the first night of Passover.

Sefer Torah – Torah scroll.

Shabbat – the Sabbath.

Shechinah – Divine Presence.

Shiva – Lit. "seven" – reference to the seven day mourning period.

Glossary

Shema – "Hear O Israel" prayer.

Siddur – Prayer book.

Taharat Hamishpachah – Laws of Family Purity.

Tallit Katan – Small prayer shawl.

Talmud – a voluminous compendium of Torah oral tradition.

Tanya – Source text of Chabad; written by Rabbi Shneur Zalman of Liadi (1745-1812).

Tefillin – Phylacteries.

Teshuvah – Repentance.

Tisha B'Av – The ninth day of the Hebrew month of *Av* – a national fast day commemorating the destruction of the Temples in Jerusalem.

Torah – The overall body of Jewish religious teachings; scriptural and rabbinic.

Tzedakah – Charity.

Tzitzit – Fringes worn on the corner of a square garment.

Yeshiva – Torah academy.

Yiddishkeit – Torah-Judaism.

Yisrael – Lit. "Israel"; The Jewish People.

Yomtov – Festival.

Zohar – early Kabbalistic text written by Rabbi Shimon Bar Yochai.